# THOMAS KINKADE

*Painter of Light*

Member # 10886

# THOMAS KINKADE

## Painter of Light

Text by
Manny Skolnick
and
Thomas Kinkade

Design by
Charlotte Kay

LIGHTPOST PUBLISHING, SAN JOSE, CALIFORNIA

*Dedicated to my family*
*and all families*

−Thomas Kinkade 1993−

## ACKNOWLEDGEMENTS

I would like to thank the following people for their hard work and efforts in producing this book: Cheryl Sanchez, my personal assistant; Jean Sweeney, production coordinator; Charlotte Kay, for her beautiful design work; Manny Skolnick, for capturing art in words; and Hal Belmont for pulling it all together.

I would especially like to thank my friend and partner Ken Raasch, for his faith in me since the beginning and his ever widening vision; and Linda Raasch for her enthusiasm, intelligence and support.

I'd like to thank Dan Byrne, Sue Edstrom, Thom Lange, Gary Wimp, Paul Barboza, Donna Pace, Brent Higginson, Bud Peterson, Kevin Leapley, and all the other talented and dedicated people of Media Arts Group and Lightpost Publishing. You are the people whose hard work and dedication has made possible the vision of enriching people's lives through art.

I offer my heartfelt appreciation to the numerous art galleries, gift shops, dealers and regional representatives who work so hard on a daily basis sharing my art with others. Thank you for your love and support.

To the collectors who honor me with their kind words of encouragement and their enthusiasm, for including my art in their lives, I say from the deepest part of me: Thank you and God bless you.

And, of course, I offer my love and thanks to my wife, Nanette and my daughters, Merritt and Chandler who have kept me balanced, confident, and creative throughout the years. Through their encouragement, warmth and wisdom, I have been able to paint paintings that will bring joy to others.

Finally, and most importantly, I thank my heavenly father, who through Christ has given me new life and continues to bless me beyond what I could ask or think.

*Second Printing 1994*
ISBN 0-9638635-0-9

Printed and bound in Korea.

# CONTENTS

*And God said, "Let there be light,"*
*and there was light. God saw that*
*the light was good, and He separated*
*the light from the darkness.*

—Genesis 1:3-4

# THOMAS KINKADE
## The Artist and His World

The sun is not yet up, and already a group of about fifty people has begun lining up in front of the cold steel door of the auditorium. The air is chilly and the more experienced hands have come prepared with blankets and woolen caps. Three hours later, at nine a.m., the line has stretched to about two hundred people. Folding chairs and cribbage boards dot the line and wrinkled newspapers are passed from hand to hand. A sense of excitement and anticipation twinkles in the eyes of those present. Neighbors in line begin conversations. New friendships are made. Laughter crackles intermittently through the crowd. An annual tradition is in progress.

By late afternoon the earlybirds have settled in. Though still in good spirits, many lean back in their folding chairs or recline on blankets. The morning group has been joined by many more as the line burgeons to several thousand patient souls. The smoke of portable barbecues fills the air as many enjoy an outdoor lunch in line. The atmosphere is that of a festival or celebration. By now the line stretches from the door of the auditorium through the neighboring parking lot and alongside the road for a distance of many blocks. Though for many the wait has lasted nearly half a day, no sense of frustration or discouragement is evident. Many do this every year. Entire offices close for the day so employees can be there. Plans that would require people to be out of the area on that day are adjusted. Kids are sent to baby-sitters or taken out of school to be part of the line.

"I wouldn't miss it." says one.

Another says, "Four years ago I missed it. I've regretted it ever since."

A third person adds, "Next year I'm bringing my RV so I can get in line a day early and be first."

The buzz of the line intensifies as the big moment nears.

At five o'clock the doors will open. The crowd is stirring anxiously. At five o'clock the wait will be over. At five o'clock...

Is this the line for some long-awaited concert by the latest superstar? Perhaps the entry gates to a hotly contested annual sporting event, or maybe the last night of a Broadway show? None of these. In fact, the truth may seem a bit surprising, for it is not sports, or music, or even drama that has brought out the crowds today. It is art. For on this day, the crowd has arrived to purchase copies of a new print being released by an artist whose uplifting, light filled creations are cherished by hundreds of thousands annually. An artist who enjoys an almost unprecedented level of success and public admiration, yet remains humbly committed to the enduring values of faith, family and home.

The artist's name is Thomas Kinkade.

## PORTRAIT OF THE ARTIST

Thomas Kinkade doesn't usually do portraits. And yet, this collection of his work can best be understood as an extended self-portrait. You won't see much of the artist in his paintings; Kinkade appears reluctantly and modestly in his work when he appears at all. Yet the art is personal and revealing nonetheless. As you page through this rich and wonderful gallery of Kinkade art, you will meet the artist's family, enjoy his wry humor, share his sense of adventure, become his travelling companion. Better still, you will savor the myriad beauties of the commonplace as seen through his eyes and be touched by the power of his faith.

*Inspiration for any artist, daughters Chandler (left) and Merritt are a constant delight for Thomas Kinkade.*

In the world of Thomas Kinkade, there is a wonderful harmony between his art and his life, as if the two were partners in an intricate dance.

As the artist puts it, *"I don't see my art as something distinct and different from my life. My art is nothing more than a reflection of who I am as a person—what I value and believe."*

Call it the Kinkade style. Call it his world view. Call it a kind of artistic faith. The point is that to understand the art of Thomas Kinkade fully, it is necessary to know something about the man behind the art. For that reason these opening pages will offer a brief portrait of who Thomas Kinkade is as a person and how it is that he has come to be an artist whose works stir the imaginations and touch the hearts of millions.

## A DAY IN THE LIFE OF THOMAS KINKADE

Today the artist rises with the sun. Kinkade delights in the play of sunlight and shadow; the rhythms of his life are tied more closely than most to the moods and movements of the sun. This morning he treats himself to a sunrise and is rewarded with a brilliant display of crimsons and golds filtered through the misty coastal dew that rises from the Pacific to glisten on the leaves and flowers of his home town's well-manicured yards.

"Lamplight Lane", the Kinkade family home in the coastal foothills of northern California, awakens with the dawn. The secluded retreat, nestled in lush gardens behind a lamppost-flanked brick gateway, is named after a favorite painting. The painting, appropriately enough, is a centerpiece in the Kinkade family's extensive art collection.

The early morning house rings with the laughter of children as daughters Merritt and Chandler prepare to have breakfast with Dad. Excited by plans that include a visit to papa's studio later in the afternoon, the little girls pick unenthusiastically at their bowls of steaming oatmeal. Kinkade sits in wide-eyed attention to his daughters' vivid descriptions of their plans for the day. His eyes twinkle; perhaps it is the spark of understanding from an adult who has a large dose of childhood's amazement still in him.

*"Nothing gets the creative juices flowing like a beautiful sunrise,"* says Kinkade, *"or the excitement of children eager to greet a new day. The more I progress as an artist, the more I realize I'm in the business of capturing on canvas the childlike wonder we all feel at times."*

## TWEED CAP AND BICYCLE

He makes a nostalgic picture. His trademark tweed cap set at a jaunty angle, Thomas Kinkade boards his vintage five-speed bike for a leisurely ride to his studio in the village. The path winds gradually down from the verdant coastal foothills, past the cozy bungalows and Victorian homes that make this hillside community an architectural treasure. He rides past joggers and bicyclists and whole families out for early morning exercise, then past the park where Tom and Nanette bring the girls to play,

**Aboard his bicycle,** *Thomas Kinkade winds his way to his studio in the village.*

and past new friends, who smile and wave at the now familiar sight of the artist on his bicycle.

*"Norman Rockwell was in the habit of bike riding, so I think I'm in good company,"* says the artist. *"I find my morning bike ride is a great time for warming up the brain and gathering inspiration. It's as though I'm a sponge, soaking up every sight like I'd never seen it before. A lot of painting ideas are born in the morning."*

In a sense, Thomas Kinkade is just one of many professionals heading out to another day at the office and by no means the only one to choose a bicycle for transportation. But while most of the drivers, joggers, and bicyclists will settle into a professional routine of investment counseling, business deals, or filling teeth, Kinkade is about to enter his own private world of tranquility and enchanting discoveries. And better yet, he gets to share that world with others by creating richly detailed paintings and prints.

## A RETREAT FOR THE IMAGINATION

The Kinkade studio is an intensely private place, a place where the special magic of imagination is given full encouragement. It is a fascinating place to visit, for the studio seems an outgrowth of the bubbling enthusiasm and energy of its occupant. The organized clutter that covers most surfaces has as its focal point the artist's massive easel, an imposing wood and steel object designed by Kinkade with heavy-duty performance as the obvious goal. Beginning at the base of the easel a veritable lava flow of papers, sketches, old photos, books, models and audio tapes cascades in every direction. Though an assistant occasionally stems the flow of professional debris, the artist's working habits are so intense that any attempt at tidiness is overwhelmed by the ongoing rush of creative energy.

*"A great art critic once told me that he felt artists had an innate need to dominate their studio environment through clutter,"* Kinkade comments. *"In my case clutter is just a natural outgrowth of the long hours I put in at the studio. As I work, the painting is my only focus. I have this urgent need to work on it. Anything used in creating the painting is reached for. Anything not needed is discarded, usually on the floor. I don't even notice the space around me— my only goal is making the painting. It's as though I'm living inside the painting and not in the studio."*

The studio also boasts enormous windows and a first-class audio system, though instead of music Kinkade often prefers to listen to full-length tapes of recorded novels as he paints.

*"I love a good story,"* he says. *"In fact, I think my art has a very definite story-telling quality. To have contact with one of the great minds through books can be so inspirational to me as an artist. There's nothing like listening to a reading from Dickens while I'm painting a Victorian Christmas scene to put me in the mood."*

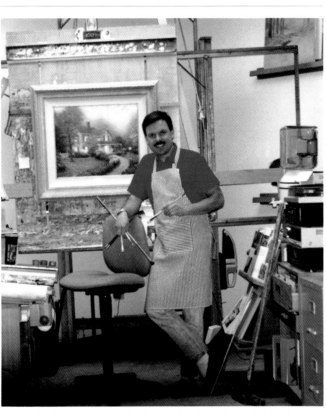

**A private sanctuary** *for the imagination, Thomas Kinkade's studio is cluttered with the evidence of artistic work.*

## A PRIVATE ART BELOVED BY MILLIONS

Though Thomas Kinkade views his studio as a very private retreat, and though few people outside of his wife, children and a small circle of close friends are ever allowed access to the sanctuary, still there is another side to the coin, a very public side. Somehow, the romantic visions, the very personal evocations of mood and place that Thomas Kinkade achieves in his art, speak to people. A lot of people.

As Kinkade prepares to put the finishing touches on his latest canvas, he senses the presence of multitudes in the studio. All manner of art lovers and collectors, perhaps millions, will ultimately have the chance to view, admire, and collect this most public of private artworks. Thomas Kinkade's art has become an expression and reflection of many dreams, an artistic ministry of hope to a large and growing congregation.

*"You do things as a painter for very private, artistic reasons,"* Kinkade says. *"You have to. And then it turns out that something public is happening—lives are being touched by your art. In a way you have to ignore that. As an artist you must continue to reach deep inside yourself to the private inner daydreams we all share. Making those daydreams come alive on canvas will bring joy to others. But it must bring joy to you first."*

## EARLY YEARS

If "family" and "home" are foundational aspects of Thomas Kinkade's art, perhaps it is an outgrowth of the close-knit family he grew up in and the old-fashioned small town that was his boyhood home.

Thomas Kinkade grew up in Placerville, a small town in the foothills of northern California. The Kinkade family has Scotch-Irish roots and, though financially poor, was rich in the greatest form of wealth: a nurturing and affirming love. Tom's mother valued culture and constantly encouraged her young son's growing talent. She even framed his childhood drawings and used them to decorate the family home.

As Kinkade puts it, " *I think my mother was my first 'collector'. Seeing my drawings hanging on the wall next to reproductions of great masterpieces by Rembrandt and Van Gogh first suggested to me that I might become an artist myself someday. My mother was a visionary; I thank God for her encouragement.*"

In addition to his mother, Kinkade remembers the support given by his older sister, Kate, who seemed at times like a second mother, helping him with homework and constantly bringing home art books from her job at the town library. His younger brother Pat was a catalyst for Tom's creativity, for the two shared a childhood full of humor and imagination. His father also played a role in Kinkade's developing talent, for Tom's dad frequently took him to meet

*Venice Canal, 10" x 8" oil on canvas (outdoor sketch)*

established professionals in the field; professionals who universally gave the young man the same message: "You're going to be an artist someday!"

Kinkade remembers his boyhood as having a Tom Sawyer-like quality filled with elaborate tree forts and clubhouses, with improvised soapbox derbies and long bike rides, with nighttime visits to spooky old houses, and with mischievous stunts and endeavors.

"*My brother Pat was my partner in crime,*" Kinkade remembers. "*Together, there was no dare we wouldn't take, no adventure we wouldn't embrace. Our tree house was a makeshift palace in the air. We had secret hideouts and home-made go-carts—and of course, an entire cast of imaginary characters in our nightly skits. I grew up in a place and time when six and seven year olds could ride their bikes to town by themselves without their parents having to worry. It was a very innocent era.*"

The story of Thomas Kinkade the artist begins with the talent, which seemed evident virtually from birth. As a child, Kinkade was something of an artistic prodigy. By the age of four his drawings displayed a grasp of depth and detail, as well as a remarkable richness of imagination.

His mother may have been the first to recognize Tom's talent, but she was by no means the last. Kinkade was an extraordinary academic student, but it soon became clear to teachers that his artistic gift was little short of amazing.

As he progressed through the early grades, Kinkade found encouragement from teacher after teacher. Interestingly enough, many of the teachers who supported Kinkade's developing abilities have resurfaced as he has become known, occasionally surprising him at his public appearances.

Even the other children in the neighborhood acknowledged Tom's unique gifts as an artist. Kinkade remembers with a chuckle:

*"Other kids were known for their ability to stand on their head or throw a ball, but I was always known as the kid who could draw."*

## THE APPRENTICE FINDS HIS MASTERS

*"I think that a person is truly blessed if he finds one great mentor in a lifetime. I've had two."*

So says Thomas Kinkade about two talented men who greatly shaped his artistic life during his formative teenage years. Though Kinkade believes all artists are essentially self-taught, he is quick to acknowledge an immense debt to the two men who acted as directional pointers for his developing artistic life. The first was Charles Bell, who Kinkade met while working a summer job in a local sign shop. In his sixties, but blessed with the vigor, energy, and restless talents of a much younger man, Charles Bell taught the twelve year old Kinkade much more than the art of sign painting. A bit of a "renaissance man", Bell was a wonderfully able boat designer, engineer, and author, as well as a sign painter and talented artist. He opened up exciting vistas of potential achievement for the eager boy. Above all, Charles Bell, or "Charlie"

*Puerto Vallarta, 8" x 10" oil on canvas (outdoor sketch)*

as Tom remembers him, drove home the need for discipline and hard work if an artist is ever to realize his gifts.

*"Charlie worked incredibly hard and lived a very disciplined life,"* says Kinkade. *"I think my strong work ethic dates back to him."*

Kinkade's second mentor was Glenn Wessels, Professor Emeritus at the University of California and former head of its prestigious art department. This master teacher, a contemporary of such luminaries as Picasso, Gertrude Stein, Braque, Hemingway, and Ansel Adams, and a giant in the world of Twentieth Century art in his own right, became a neighbor at the most propitious moment, selecting the old barn next to the Kinkade home for his studio.

Kinkade quickly acknowledges the miraculous hand of God in the uncanny coincidence of a master artist/teacher settling next door: *"It was as though God was sovereignly providing for my education as an artist."*

Thomas Kinkade was sixteen, charged with energy and ambition. Wessels was nearly eighty, and an injury suffered in a jeep trip with famed photographer and close friend Ansel Adams had slowed him down. For two years, Kinkade stepped into the breach, performing all manner of chores in the studio, from washing floors to stretching and preparing canvas. At the same time, the young apprentice soaked up Wessels' vast experience and fascinating ideas about art. The old professor believed that art is a high calling, and that artists, not politicians, are the innovators and indeed, the true leaders of society. For Kinkade this was fuel to the fire for his already developing convictions about his role as an artist.

*"I remember the anticipation as I went to that studio each day,"* remembers Kinkade. *"I would crack open the door and see Glenn at work on a new canvas. I can still smell the intoxicating scent of the studio—a mixture of turpentine and brewing coffee!*

*"Glenn loved opening up dusty volumes of art history and studying the compositions. We would discuss the merits of a particular painting for hours. Often he would just sit and muse about his life— his years in Paris during the period between the wars, his memories of sketching trips across the Alps on skis with his wife, the eccentricities of the great artists he had known over the years. I hung on every word he said. Somehow he was defining for me the exciting possibilities of life as an artist. He taught me not so much how to paint, but rather why to paint."*

## TAKING THE BOY OUT OF THE COUNTRY: COLLEGE YEARS

*"The move from the rural tranquility of Placerville to the bustling activity of U.C. Berkeley was nothing less than culture shock,"* says Kinkade. *"Of course, this was the mid-Seventies and the frenzied politics of the Sixties were a thing of the past. But the social and intellectual ferment at Berkeley was as vigorous as ever, and I came to value the challenge, the excitement, the sense of possibility."*

Thomas Kinkade seems always to have possessed a spiritual and aesthetic compass. On the huge and daunting Berkeley campus several times as populous as his home town, he moved confidently in his own direction of artistic growth and self-discovery. In another

**Deep in thought,** *Thomas Kinkade during his college years, at work in his Golden Palms studio.*

"miraculous coincidence", Kinkade was assigned as his dorm roommate the enormously talented James Gurney, now well known for his famous "Dinotopia" creations. Gurney would become a frequent artistic collaborator and Kinkade's closest artist friend.

While a student at Berkeley, Kinkade found work that furthered his art, becoming cartoonist and illustrator for the *Daily Californian* and earning the then proud sum of $3 per comic strip and $5 per illustration. As Kinkade humorously recalls, the editor's calculations of wages must have been based on an estimate that Kinkade could turn out an illustration in an hour or less.

He obtained a studio in the basement of a nearby apartment house which became a seedbed for the researches into landscape and effects of pictorial light that laid the foundation for Kinkade's mature style. Also, at the close by Oakland Museum, Kinkade discovered the epic landscape paintings that would become his lifelong inspiration.

*"I remember the first time I stepped into the great hall of the Oakland Museum,"* says Kinkade. *"Here were all these magnificent traditional landscape paintings. I stood in front of Thomas Hill's great painting of Yosemite Valley and I was absolutely awestruck. I said to myself, 'I want to do paintings like this.'"*

From Berkeley we move to what is perhaps the most rigorous artistic training ground in America, the Art Center College of Design in Pasadena. The curriculum is demanding, the atmosphere intensely competitive, the students nothing less than brilliant. In an arena of stars, Thomas Kinkade soon established himself as one of the superstars.

*"I was a bit of a rebel at Art Center,"* Kinkade remembers. *"Everyone was doing all this hard edged stuff, but I wanted to paint soft, romantic things. A few of my teachers, especially Ted Youngkin and Jack Leynwood, encouraged my traditional approach. I definitely had my own way of doing things."*

With its offer of cheap lodging not far from school, The Golden Palms apartments had become a haven for ambitious Art Center students and an island of creative effort in the midst of urban L.A. Kinkade became a part of the inspired circle of artists who lived at the Golden Palms, a group which had become a sort of private club or fraternity of artists. This unorthodox gathering of talented individuals included Kinkade, James Gurney, Paul Chadwick, Ron Harris, and Bryn Barnard each destined to become a star painter, cartoonist, fantasy artist or author in his own right. The atmosphere was charged with energy and excitement, impromptu sketch sessions and improvised dramatic skits were the order of the day. The comraderie has lasted a lifetime; the influential artistic bond that grew up at the Art Center and the Golden Palms remains vibrant—a kind of modern-day Pre-Raphaelite Brotherhood.

*"An artist's most important education comes not from school, but from the stimulating company of fellow artists,"* says Kinkade. *"My relationship with the other G.P. (Golden Palms) artists set the tone for my career. We challenged each other to dream big dreams and to dare to accomplish them. And in the process we had a lot of fun."*

**Walking the rails**, *Thomas Kinkade and James Gurney search for a new subject during their cross-country trip.*

## AN ARTIST COMES OF AGE

Growing in Thomas Kinkade during his Golden Palms and Art Center years was a thirst for adventure and outdoor painting that has subsequently become a life pattern.

*"I felt like I needed to get away from the confines of the classroom and into the open air,"* says Kinkade. *"It was about this time that Jim Gurney and I began to develop the concept of the 'hoist.'"*

The "hoist" as Kinkade and Gurney still refer to it, is a sketching adventure strictly for the bold and the reckless.

*"I'm not sure why we called it a hoist,"* Kinkade recalls, *"but when one of us said to the other, 'Let's go hoisting', we knew just what we meant."* And what they meant was, *"Pack your paints and sketchbooks, lets hit the road!"*

Their travels took them to locations both seedy and sublime, picturesque and pathetic. They would set up paints and palettes on mountaintops, in the desert, at freight yards and bus stops. On one of these "hoists" the daring young artists met Bud, a man who would quite inadvertently change their lives. Bud was a professional hobo, a philosopher of the Jack Kerouak school, a glorious spinner of yarns, a true American original. As the young artists sketched away, Bud described the intricate subculture of hoboing in richly poetic terms, extolling the "music of the rails." The hobo-philosopher had planted a seed; Kinkade and Gurney decided to set out on the most glorious "hoist" of all: a coast-to-coast tour of America by rail.

Dressed identically in surplus-store gas station attendant uniforms, with their art gear packed in oversized backpacks, the adventuresome artists hit the rails the following summer. And then, a strange thing happened. The country began to take notice of their exploits. The "hobo artists" as they were christened by the media, would no sooner pull into a town and begin to talk with the locals, than someone would point them to the newspaper office or radio station. From Yuma, Arizona to Nashville, Tennessee they were the subjects of feature newspaper articles. In Wichita, Kansas, they spent an hour on the radio discussing their adventures.

Kinkade and Gurney soon realized that they'd stumbled onto something. Their unique combination of art and adventure had touched a sympathetic chord in an America searching for meaning and a return to simpler, common sense values, the kind expressed in earlier eras by Will Rogers and Mark Twain.

An idea struck them: Why not write a book about this? Arriving in Manhattan, the pair took their last remaining funds and rented a typewriter. They hammered out a rough draft of a manuscript proposal, gathered up their sketches and headed to the biggest publisher of art related books, Watson/Guptill of New York. And, in yet another "miracle", Watson/Guptill liked the idea.

*"We walked into this huge publishing house with crew cut haircuts and shirts stained by the grease of the rails."* Kinkade remembers, *"They probably figured, 'These guys look odd enough to actually write a good book!'"*

*The rewards of hard work— Thomas Kinkade and wife Nanette attend the opening for "Fire and Ice."*

When the book finally appeared in 1982, the publisher's faith was affirmed: *The Artist's Guide to Sketching* became one of the best selling art books of the season, and Kinkade and Gurney had become Watson/Guptill's youngest published authors.

While writing the book, Kinkade landed a job as a background painter for the major animated feature, *Fire and Ice*, directed by noted Hollywood iconoclast Ralph Bakshi, with art direction by the legendary fantasy painter Frank Frazetta. Working ten hour shifts on the movie, Kinkade painted some 600 scenic backgrounds in a frenetic two year period. During this time, Thomas Kinkade began mastering the techniques that would eventually win him recognition as the *"Painter of Light"*.

With a major motion picture and well-received art book to his credit, Kinkade had yet to reach his 25th birthday.

## Family Values

During those foundational years of his early twenties, another important aspect of Thomas Kinkade's life was unfolding. The saga began many years earlier when the teenaged artist met the young woman who would eventually become his wife. At age thirteen, the always ambitious Kinkade was a paperboy for a local paper as well as being an aspiring young artist. While delivering papers one day, Kinkade took notice of the beautiful blonde girl whose family had just moved to the neighborhood. Not only was she charming, witty, intelligent and beautiful, but she had a trampoline, a major asset at that age! What followed was a long, lovely summer during which the couple literally bounced their way into an innocent romance.

Following that summer, when a dozen intervening years failed to bounce her out of his heart, Thomas Kinkade did the only possible thing; he proposed to his childhood sweetheart. He and Nanette were married in 1982 in a historic chapel near their home town of Placerville.

After finishing his work on the motion picture *Fire and Ice,* the sentimental couple decided on a major move: they would return to their home town roots and relocate in Placerville. There, much like Glenn Wessels before him, Thomas Kinkade built himself a wonderful studio in a remodeled barn. The years brought two lovely daughters to their family: Merritt (born June 14, 1988) and Chandler (born March 8, 1991). The children have been a source of inspiration to Kinkade ever since.

Kinkade puts it this way, *"Nanette and the kids are the center of my life. They are truly my greatest blessings from God. When I'm away from them I feel as though I left part of me behind. Their support provides balance to my busy life as an artist."*

Family, first and foremost, means the wife and children who play such a vital role in Kinkade's life, as in his art. Family also means the playful sense of humor Kinkade honed as a child and now displays in his art. His paintings often feature multiple tributes to his family: initials, birth dates, hearts, holiday dates, Christmas wreathes, and of course the famous hidden "N" Kinkade distributes throughout his paintings as a tribute to his wife Nanette. This last element has become

***Wedding bells and smiles,*** *the artist and his new bride, Nanette, on their wedding day— May 2, 1982*

something of a tradition. Tom even includes a small number beside his signature denoting the number of hidden "N"s in that particular painting.

In Kinkade's mind his family is also an extension of his personal faith. Two years before he married Nanette, Thomas Kinkade made a commitment to putting God at the center of his life, turning his life and career over to the direction of his creator.

*"When I met Christ in 1980, I asked the Lord to direct my career,"* says Kinkade. *"Since then he's opened many doors and closed many others. Throughout it all, I've been blessed."*

## THE BIRTH OF A COMPANY

Following his move to Placerville in 1983, Kinkade's horizons literally exploded, for shortly thereafter his first two prints appeared on the market. "Dawson", his first experiment in limited edition prints, was quickly snapped up by art dealers who immediately recognized the fact that a powerful new talent was now in print. A follow up print, "Placerville 1916" was a tribute to his home town's nostalgic history, and sold out almost immediately. With the funds generated by these first tentative efforts, Kinkade and his wife began producing more prints.

Kinkade remembers, *"In those early years my wife and I were just learning about making and selling prints. We did everything ourselves. I created the painting and supervised the production of the prints, while Nanette kept books and even did packing and shipping. It was a busy time, but we didn't have children yet and we were having fun working together in our business."*

A few years later, Kinkade's growing print business caught the eye of long-time friend and gifted businessman, Ken Raasch. And the rest, as they say, is history. The company that grew out of the alignment of Thomas Kinkade's extraordinary talents as an artist, and Ken Raasch's extraordinary skills as a businessman and entrepreneur has literally made art publishing history. Lightpost Publishing has become in a few short years the largest organization of its kind anywhere, with publishing and other business activities impacting markets around the world.

Kinkade marvels at the miraculous business that has developed around his art.

*"I stand amazed at how something as seemingly simple as paintings could have such a large impact on so many lives,"* muses Kinkade. *"It's inspiring to visit the offices of Lightpost Publishing and see the group of highly talented and dedicated people all committed to bringing my art and other uplifting products to people everywhere. It's also humbling, because I realize more than ever, God has surely had His hand on Lightpost."*

**In Beatrix Potter's farmyard,** *Thomas Kinkade works while daughter Merritt feeds the ducks.*

## The Travels of an Artist

His extraordinary successes over the years have allowed Kinkade the freedom to pursue his art in his own way. And a large part of Kinkade's way of making art involves constantly searching for new sources of beauty. That means travel.

Thomas Kinkade's appetite for travel seems to be never satisfied. The conviction that art and adventure go hand-in-hand has taken him far beyond the 1980 "hoist" across America, and into a lifestyle that is truly global. He is one of the relatively few artists who practice the "plein air" painting style so popular in the last century. This approach involves taking easel and canvas outdoors and creating paintings on location. This intrepid approach to picture-making has lead to some extraordinary experiences. Like the great American landscape painters Frederick Church and Albert Bierstadt before him, no location is too remote, no journey too difficult to lure Kinkade and his easel.

Kinkade has boarded bush planes loaded with survival gear and painting supplies, and has trekked through the awesome wilderness of Alaska, sketching in temperatures so cold that he had to mix his watercolors in rubbing alcohol because water would have frozen solid almost instantly. He has painted in tropical villages in heat so intense that only an umbrella shading the easel could keep him from sunstroke. Kinkade has taken shelter under a scaffold in Venice to capture the silvery light of a driving thunderstorm as lightning played above the canals. He has followed in the footsteps of Monet and Renoir, setting up his easel in the streets of Paris to capture the bustling life of the City of Lights. And, of course, he has walked the English countryside, discovering and celebrating the quiet charms of its estates and rural cottages. In a sense, the whole world has become Thomas Kinkade's studio.

"*I especially love to travel in places where the culture is many centuries old,*" comments Kinkade. "*In California, any structure that's a hundred years old is considered an historical site. In Europe and other places, anything that recent is little more than a nuisance, interfering with one's enjoyment of the real antiquities. I like old things that have the mark of history on them; they're incredibly rich with human dreams. I'm especially drawn to tumbledown buildings and cottages that seem to me to possess personalities as distinctive as their inhabitants.*"

Tom and Nanette feel especially blessed to be able to take daughters Merritt and Chandler along on many of their travels. While growing up, the artist's family had little opportunity to travel due to the poor state of their finances. Now, as an adult, Kinkade's frequent travels are a special gift he feels fortunate to offer his children. How exciting it is for Tom to load his daughters in a stroller and wander the country lanes of an English village, or to sit at a sidewalk cafe in Paris and watch his children marvel at the strange words spoken by passersby.

As he puts it, "*The broad horizons that come from experiencing other cultures is something I never had as a child. I'm thankful that my children will grow up with insight into other lands and other peoples. Besides, discovering beauty in faraway places is a major part of my inspiration as an artist.*"

***In the footsteps of Monet,*** *Thomas Kinkade paints on the busy streets of Paris.*

## More Than Talent— The Qualities of Kinkade's Art

To understand the art of Thomas Kinkade, acknowledging his prodigious talent is only chapter one. Beyond talent are the issues of timeless quality, of personal values, even individual wisdom. That is particularly true of an artist like Kinkade, noted for his vibrancy of spirit and gregarious outlook on life, who not only shares his experiences and sense of beauty through his art, but who shares his uplifting ideology and intense personal faith as well.

But how could we describe the uncanny, almost hypnotic appeal of a Thomas Kinkade painting? What is it that explains his meteoric rise to the heights of his profession, or the entrancing charm of his creations? The paintings of Thomas Kinkade seem to possess qualities so compelling that people are willing to wait in line for hours to acquire them or will gladly spend much of their discretionary income to build collections often numbering 10, 20, even 100 pieces or more.

One aspect of the appeal of Kinkade's work must certainly be its technical mastery. Thomas Kinkade is one of the greatest craftsmen of traditional oil painting technique alive today. His works are, simply put, masterpieces. That is to say, they are pieces created by a true living master of the art of applying paint to canvas. Examine a Kinkade original and you will see layer upon layer of carefully modulated pigment. The effect is mystifying, and begs the question, "How was this done?"

This is by design, for as Kinkade puts it, *"I desire to create an effect that is not easily understandable. I use many layers of paint, carving and shaping the pigment like a sculptor would carve marble. Some layers are thick, some are thin. When the painting is completed, all the layers have been woven together like a tapestry, so that when you see it you simply notice the subject, not the way it was painted."*

Another key to the appeal of Kinkade's art is his mastery of composition. Kinkade's paintings draw you into the world he has created and make you want to stay there. His sense of composition has a very theatrical feel to it, perhaps because of his work in the movie industry. It's almost as though he's the director of a film, creating a mood, establishing the setting and arranging the lighting.

*"I like to think of my paintings as windows for the imagination,"* says Kinkade. *"I want you to enter my painting and feel at peace."*

A third, and perhaps the most obvious, reason for the enchanting appeal of a Thomas Kinkade painting is his incomparable mastery of light and its effects. Kinkade's paintings literally *radiate with light*. In fact, the effect is so commanding that visitors to galleries displaying Kinkade's works are often stopped dead in their tracks by the illusion of light. The effect is not the result of any technical gimmick, florescent paints or the like, but is simply an outpouring of Thomas Kinkade's innate sensitivity to dramatic effects of light,

**In the footsteps of his hero,** Thomas Kinkade at work in Norman Rockwell's studio. Kinkade was priviledged in 1992 to paint professionally in the famous Arlington, Vermont studio.

combined with his outstanding mastery of traditional techniques for suggesting light through color mixtures.

*"Light is essential to all art, for by it we see form. What is different about my approach is that I enhance the effects of light subtlely to empower the emotional effect of the canvas,"* says Kinkade. *"This is consistent with my spiritual values—after all Christ described Himself as 'the Light of the world'. If you study scripture to any degree you will soon see that 'light' is consistent with God's nature, while 'darkness' is not. I want my work to in some small way bring light to people's lives—there's enough darkness out there already."*

But the art of Thomas Kinkade is also loved for another, possibly more subtle reason: deep, life-affirming humanity. Like the works of his lifelong hero Norman Rockwell, Kinkade's paintings proclaim the value and dignity of humankind. Through gentle whimsy and a joyous celebration of beauty, Kinkade's subjects somehow strike a nerve with young and old, simple and sophisticated, rich and poor. For all people everywhere share the same simple aspirations, the same foundations to life: family, home, a quest for peace and a love of nature's beauty.

*"I reject the idea of art for art's sake."* Kinkade comments, *"I firmly believe that art serves larger ends than that. I want to serve others through my work, because I care about and love people. In fact, I choose my landscapes, my cottages, my cityscapes precisely because*

*they reveal so much about people. The best portrait of a family can be the home where they live or the garden they cultivate. And the best portrait of a nation can be the look and the life of its cities and villages. I try to affirm the value of life and the value of humanity in my work. I try to remind people that there's still good things out there, that there's still hope. Perhaps that's why people frequently tell me that my paintings have become a source of inspiration in their lives."*

## A Studio Visit

Inspiration. A common word around the studio of an artist humbly aware of the source of his own inspiration and deeply serious about the role his work plays in the lives of others. Kinkade has been thinking about this subject a lot lately. Which returns us to the present moment. Thomas Kinkade sits alone in his studio, a tape of Dickens' *David Copperfield* is on the cassette player, the current canvas is on his easel. He considers the addition of a silvery hint of dew to the leaves of a distant tree. Yes, perfect. It's finished.

A knock at the door. A tiny but insistent knock that he's come to recognize. Kinkade smiles. It's Chandler's knock; Nanette and the girls have come to visit the studio.

*"My life is certainly busy, but I never let the urgent things come before the important things."* Kinkade notes, *"The public can be demanding; success of any sort has its own special challenges. But if I thought that all the trappings of my professional life were interfering with my walk with the Lord or my life with my family, then I'd make*

*drastic changes. But thankfully my work and the rest of my life blend beautifully together. In fact, in my mind I don't separate the two."*

The girls make themselves at home in the artist's studio. In fact, Kinkade has set up a special canvas, with brushes and paint, for their amusement. Merritt and Chandler, in turn, will apply paint to the canvas. Occasionally daddy will let them work a bit on his painting. Once or twice he's even incorporated a few of their brush strokes into a finished piece.

*"I don't know if my daughters will become professional artists."*

*Near Seal Rock, 12' x 16' oil on canvas (outdoor sketch)*

Kinkade observes, *"That, of course, is a question of inclination, of their special talents. But I am sure that they will be comfortable around art; they'll understand its aims and appreciate its execution. That is a gift I'm determined to give them."*

Today Nanette will scrutinize the canvas. "That tree looks a little too skinny," she observes as she studies the current work on the easel. Since the beginning of their marriage, Nanette has been one of the few people allowed to comment on works in progress. She's developed an amazing facility to visualize where the painting is going and to notice things Kinkade may have overlooked. Tom agrees with her assessment and hurriedly scribbles a reminder to make the change. Noise from another room reminds the mother that it's about nap time. After the inevitable hugs and kisses, Nanette and the girls stroll the mile or so back to home. Kinkade resumes working, quickly making the recommended changes. Before he leaves the studio tonight another work, which he hopes will bring joy to countless people, will be complete.

## CELEBRATION

The Kinkades have a kind of ceremony with which they welcome a new artwork into the "family". Nanette prepares a candlelit dinner, served outdoors under starlight. A linen cloth covers the wrought iron lawn table; candles flicker and glow in an ornate candelabra. Dressed comfortably but well, Tom and Nanette survey the table. A sense of tongue-in-cheek formality pervades. Nanette giggles at Tom's overly dramatic speech celebrating the event. The girls splash and frolic in the cool waters of the nearby pool, and emerge, dripping, to eat their dinner on paper plates. The darkness that settles over Lamplight Lane is comforting;

the sky is ablaze with stars. It is quiet and the moment is peaceful. Thomas Kinkade looks into the eyes of those he loves, and realizes anew what a blessed man he is.

It is a lovely picture of a family secure in its values, strong in its love and faith. A picture reflected in countless variations, in the heartfelt, life-enriching paintings of Thomas Kinkade.

There can be no more satisfying conclusion to our narrative than this image of the Kinkade family, at their ease, celebrating art and life. We join the artist in inviting you to enjoy the more important part of this extended self-portrait: the marvelous gallery of Kinkade art that awaits you in this book.

Manny Skolnick
Summer, 1993

*The Kinkade Family at home at Lamplight Lane.*

# THOMAS KINKADE'S

## Gardens and Landscapes of Light

The original garden of light was, of course, Eden, which I imagine to be a perfect expression of the divine plan in its abundant fertility, its delightful profusion of colors and shapes, its fragrance, its chorus of birdsong, its gentle breezes, its grace and harmony, and its tranquil moods.

Natural vistas and tended gardens are imperfect memories of Eden. In the wild places, I find a joyous exuberance in the bursts of color of a blooming field in springtime, or in autumn's flaming leaves. Gardens charm me with their sense of order, their artful arrangement of nature's colors and textures, their planned variety. I greatly admire the gardener's patient faith that nature can be tamed, controlled, even improved by the imposition of human judgement and design. The gardens that I love to paint strike a balance between man and nature. They are luxuriant, brilliantly colored, spontaneous—trees, flowers, shrubs grow in splendid profusion. But they also betray subtle human touches, even such expressions of sentiment as hearts or initials wrought into iron fences or carved into the trunks of trees.

As a painter, I am in a sense, a gardener myself, but with this important difference; it doesn't take me years to train a rose bush to climb a trellis. I can create that effect with a few brushstrokes. So of course, I have the freedom to create more romantic, more imaginative gardens than real gardeners can!

Nature's lovely vistas can provide a wonderful atmosphere of peace and serenity—even when their beauty exists only on canvas. I hope that my "Gardens and Landscapes of Light" will provide that serenity for you.

# *Beside Still Waters*

There is a place I visit only in my imagination—and share with you only in my art—because any human presence would spoil its perfect tranquility. It is a wonderful hideaway, bathed in a silvery light, ablaze with flowers of every hue and description, silent save for the murmur of gently rushing waters. I'm not sure to this day whether it's a dream or a memory.

"Beside Still Waters" is my vision of what the Garden of Eden must have been like. As a Christian, I sometimes speculate on the mystery and wonder of God's creation—nature unspoiled and perfect, as it was in Eden. As an artist, I convey through my art my own wonder at the richness and variety I still find in the natural world, in the joyous energy of sunlight and growing flowers. There is a warm, animated quality to the light here. It paints the leaves of the silver birch and dances on the water.

As I worked on "Beside Still Waters", I often felt that I was trespassing on a world too perfect for people to see. Sometimes, as I applied the paint, I actually found myself holding my breath so I wouldn't disturb the silence of Eden!

*Oil on canvas, 16"x 20"*

# *Afternoon Light, Dogwood*

I've seen glorious Spring scenes like this often during my travels. I hold nature to be the most accomplished of artists, and I'm grateful for the inspirations she so generously provides.

There is a special radiance to the light in Springtime— it shimmers through the new-green leaves, and dances on the cool stone path with every breath of breeze. Flowers are exuberant, but a dogwood tree seems a crowning glory to any Spring scene.

I knew that a scene with flowers and dogwood was a perfect celebration of spring and its new beginnings. It was only after I completed "Afternoon Light, Dogwood" in my studio that I realized what a perfect expression of the season of rebirth the dogwood—the legendary source of the wood for our Lord's cross, and the symbol of Easter—truly is.

*Oil on canvas, 24"x 20"*

# The Broadwater Bridge, Thomashire

Perhaps my pleasant memories of this beautiful Victorian-era stone bridge are not entirely based on the subject itself, but are also based on the wonderful ambiance of its location. "Broadwater Bridge" spans one of the most delightful, most tranquil stretches of watercourse I've yet seen. Just beyond the bridge a spillway acts as a tiny dam to back up the normally small stream to a width of perhaps twenty or thirty yards. Flowering shrubs and lush trees line this wide part of the stream, casting dappled shade along the well mown green banks. In all directions, nothing interrupts the unbelievably pastoral beauty of the setting.

In fact, this stretch of the stream is part of what was once a large private estate which has been converted into an exclusive trout fishing club for gentlemen and ladies of ample means. For the week or so that I sat beside my easel diligently working on this painting, dapper looking people carrying fly rods would occasionally walk by, tip their tweed caps at me and say, "Oh, I say, jolly good show!" (or something equally charming) as they saw my painting. I was so thoroughly taken with the gentility and peacefulness of the location that I invited my wife and children to the spot on several occasions to picnic in the sunshine beside the stream as I painted.

*Oil on canvas, 16"x 20"*

# Entrance to the Manor House

"The Lord of the Manor"—I just love the sense of tradition behind those words. The title conveys a sense of domain and dignity that seems very British to me. I think many people have imagined life in a grand old manor house, managing estates, maintaining a wonderful stable, perhaps riding to the hounds, and of course, enjoying afternoon tea.

For these people perhaps the stately brick dwelling I've portrayed in "Entrance to the Manor House" would do nicely. Its proud facade suggests a reserved quality of the life that is very properly obscured from view. I especially like the austere simplicity of the gate and wall. The owners have entrusted nature with the task of decoration, and she has responded brilliantly with this lavish display of flowers. The collaboration between man and nature, a product of centuries, is a most attractive feature of these historic English homes.

A painting like this is an imaginative adventure for me. I try to put myself very much into a "Manor House" frame of mind while I work on paintings like this. I hope the painting will have the same effect on your imagination. Tea, anyone?

*Oil on canvas, 16"x 20"*

# *Morning Light*

**C**an the quality of light actually be the subject of a painting? Unquestionably the answer is "yes."

Nothing is more important to an artist than sunlight itself. Warm, radiant, richly shadowed, subtlely tinged with endless nuances of color, sunlight provides a wealth of atmospheric effects that no artificial light can begin to approach. In "Morning Light" a flower garden becomes a fabulous canvas onto which the morning sun paints a glowing picture. Suffused through the mist, the light dazzles with subtle flashes of color. The rainbow-hued blossoms become mirrors of this energized light; radiant bursts of color awakening to the first touch of dawnlight.

I think an artist never sees, or paints, exactly the same garden twice. Every change of season, or time of day, or cloud formation, lends the scene a special character. Conveying that character is the challenge, and I hope, the charm of "Morning Light."

*Oil on canvas, 16"x 20"*

# Studio in the Garden

An artist's studio is his most important self portrait. Studios, after all, are the places we artists do our work; more important, they're the sanctuaries where we go to seek our inspiration. They have to be functional, comfortable, and above all, stimulating.

"Studio in the Garden" is all that and more for me. This is my second studio — a romantic hideaway in the charming California village of Carmel-by-the-Sea. I've long dreamed of a second studio—a place where I could retreat for a change of scene, but still do the work I love. And my studio in Carmel is really more than that dream come true.

On lovely days I paint under the sky, with the sound of the Blue Pacific in the distance — and nothing can be more romantic than that as far as I'm concerned! Huge windows satisfy my passion for light and allow me to stay in touch with the sun's many moods. The flowers that I love surround me in a charming English garden. And, as my collectors may have noticed, in the windows of my garden studio hang paintings that are my personal favorites.

*Oil on canvas, 12" x 16"*

# The Garden of Promise

When a close friend recently lost loved ones, I was amazed to see the serenity and peace that filled his heart. It was almost as if, despite the hardship of parting, he was already anticipating the joyful reunion that lay ahead. He reminded us that he would "see them again soon."

I was so touched with the grace and hope God had given this man that I decided to do a painting as a tribute to the hope many of us share of the better life that lies ahead. I chose a garden with a rambling stone walkway climbing up through flower hedges to illustrate my theme. In my painting, as we make our way up the stony path, we seek to reach the top, where the brilliant purity of a white dogwood in the sunlight greets us with the hope of what lies beyond the gate.

There is a garden, a place of peace promised to each of us, and the gate lies open to those who wish to come in. My prayer is that my portrayal of "The Garden of Promise" will remind many of this hope that lies ahead. As one anonymous chorus puts it:

*"Beyond the gate will peace await*
*And joy to fill each heart—*
*A fragrant bower every hour*
*And love that never parts."*

*Oil on canvas, 20"x 16"*

# The Victorian Garden

To me, a painting of a garden is a chance to celebrate the joy of pure color. The subject for this painting is loosely based on a beautiful garden that was part of one of England's most grand country estates. The morning we were there, flowers and trees, vines and hedges, were all bathed in the glow of a moist, but sunny morning and the effect was wonderfully luminous. We began wandering around the extensive grounds which included meadows and a series of interlocking lakes, when we came upon a secret garden, overgrown and almost hidden. I was intrigued by the way the garden seemed so natural as though it were cultivated yet still allowed to flourish on its own. The dappled light of the flowering trees overhead made it almost irresistible as a subject.

As I explored the garden, trying to lock my first impressions firmly in my mind, I was struck by another sensation; the overwhelming fragrance of the many blooms. It was as though I had stepped into a huge expanse of fresh flowers and was utterly surrounded by blossoms. Back home in California, as I worked on the final painting, I was reminded of the delightful floral scent of that garden. Though painters usually deal with qualities of light and color, I must say, I hope this painting captures some of that fragrant bouquet on canvas.

*Oil on canvas, 24" x 30"*

# THOMAS KINKADE'S
## Cities of Light

*I* grew up in the country. I love to paint rural scenes, but I love cities, too. San Francisco, Paris, Venice, London—these are some of my favorite travel destinations. I see no contradiction in this; the extravagant variety of experience gives life its fascination.

Cities are the richest and most complex creations of a people; the character of a nation is best gauged by the look and the life of its cities. Each of the cities and towns I enjoy has its very own distinctive character—a personality expressed in its buildings, its bustling streets, the holidays it celebrates, and the humble pursuits it values.

Whether I set up my easel on the busy boulevards of Paris, along the canals of Venice, on San Francisco's hills or along the Carmel coastline, I'm looking for one thing above all—the distinctive mood unique to that location. One of the greatest compliments I receive is when people tell me one of my paintings has captured their memories of a certain place. Interestingly enough, to capture the essence of a subject often means making

drastic changes from what's there in real life. This is especially true of cities, where charm is often hidden by urban realities. But if you look hard enough, every city has its hidden beauties. I suppose that is why I enjoy painting cities so much—to experience the joy of discovering something wondrous in an unexpected place.

The quiet of nature refreshes the soul and restores peace. As an artist, I feel that one of the great blessings I can offer people through my paintings is a sense of peace. But when I paint cities and towns, my imagination ignites with the bustling spirit of human activity. Cities are a microcosm of man's creative abilities, vast living sculptures that are constantly changing, constantly moving. Colors and lights dance across my canvas as I recreate the effervescence of city life.

I feel that cities can be places of hope, places of opportunity, places of creative stimulation. I like to think that my city paintings will share with others a bit of this hope and stimulation—a bit of the energy and beauty of mankind's great gathering places.

# BOSTON

## An Evening Stroll Through the Common

Boston is a city for walking! Some ingenious person has even installed computerized machines at popular corners to disperse custom printed maps for pedestrians, complete with distances and points of interest. One of my favorite strolls is along the tree lined corridors of Boston Common and the Public Garden. One begins by passing the lake in the Public Garden where, for decades, the famous "Swan Boats" have carried lovers young and old along a fragrant summertime route framed with lawns and lush flowering hedges. From the garden, one steps across Charles Street to Boston Common, a paradise for promenaders since the 18th century.

My last visit to Boston was in the late winter. Some of the delights of the trip were the long walks I took with my wife Nanette and our two year old daughter Merritt in her stroller along the leafless lanes of Boston Common at dusk. A wet storm front was breaking up overhead one chilly evening when I got the inspiration for this painting. I was impressed by the glowing facade of the famous Park Street Church, almost like a lighthouse seen through the mist of some rocky coast. The sweet, warm fragrance of candied peanuts roasting in the sidewalk vendor's cart is a standard fixture in Boston Common, so I included a peanut vendor in my painting. The combination of myriads of glowing lights, low hanging coastal clouds, and abundant moisture that seems to coat everything in a nostalgic glow make Boston one of my favorite subjects to paint.

*Oil on canvas, 16"x 20"*

# *Placerville in the Snow*

When a subject is as familiar as a well worn pair of shoes, the artist's challenge is to make it appear as wondrous and magical as Cinderella's glass slipper. Placerville is my home town. I grew up in it; I returned to it with my wife Nanette to raise our young family; I've spent more than half of my life there. I love the place, but sometimes, as I'm walking or driving through, it seems just as comfortable and familiar as, well, an old shoe.

When I'm working on one of my annual Placerville Christmas paintings, I have to move beyond my own familiarity with the town and see it once again through fresh eyes. In this case, I utilized the power of winter and snow to transform the town and touch an everyday scene with magic. Downtown Placerville seems encrusted in diamonds; I am as entranced as the prince must have been when he looked down to discover Cinderella's glittering glass slipper.

By the way, about the time I was working on this painting, my wife Nanette and I had our first child, Merritt. I couldn't resist the family portrait that you see in the lower left of the painting. Nanette and I stroll the sidewalk while baby Merritt pokes her curious head out of the carriage. Also, the painting that appears in the window by our family group is a miniature version of the "Placerville in the Snow" painting itself; sort of a painting within a painting.

*Oil on canvas, 24"x 36"*

# CARMEL

## *Ocean Avenue on a Rainy Afternoon*

This painting is a loving tribute to the resort village of Carmel-by-the-Sea, California. In addition to boasting the world's most famous ex-mayor, Clint Eastwood, Carmel has long been a sea-side art colony and one of the most delightful scenic regions in America.

Carmel has been a favorite family retreat for many years, so naturally I was excited to finally put on canvas some of my personal feelings about the area. I chose the view looking east along Ocean Avenue at the corner of Lincoln Street. This corner affords a broad panorama of several of the characteristics that make Carmel picturesque: Monterey pine trees, flowering hedges, and charming architecture. The corner also hosts the Pine Inn, one of Carmel's landmark lodging houses, which can be seen dominating the left-hand side of the painting. I chose a breezy afternoon with sunlight breaking after a rain in order to suggest the moisture in the air which I find so lovely about Carmel. Also, since Carmel has always been so reminiscent of a European village, I couldn't resist posing my wife Nanette aboard her bicycle making her way down the misty avenue with a basket full of French bread in back of her.

*Oil on canvas, 24"x 36"*

# CARMEL

## Dolores Street and The Tuck Box Tea Room

Besides the Tuck Box Tea Room, famous for delicious English scones, Dolores Street features many other Carmel landmarks which make for a charming stroll on a rainy afternoon. The mood on Dolores Street is a combination of timelessness and hustle-bustle. I tried to capture these aspects in my latest tribute to my favorite coastal village this side of England.

Interestingly enough, as I was at work on this Carmel painting, I received word that the print of my earlier Carmel painting, "Carmel, Ocean Avenue on a Rainy Afternoon", had completely sold out. On further discussions with my publisher,

I was gratified to learn that my first Carmel print had been popular everywhere, not just in the region of Carmel. This proves my long held belief that beauty is universal, no matter what the specific location is.

It may also prove what a Carmel gallery owner once told me regarding the worldwide scope of visitors to the area: "No matter where you live, if you travel, you'll eventually come to Carmel." I hope my newest Carmel print will bring a bit of the charm and energy of one of America's most quaint villages to people all over, whether they come to Carmel or not!

*Oil on canvas, 20"x 24"*

# NEW YORK

## Sixth Avenue and Central Park South

That a kid from rural Northern California should have come to love New York City may seem improbable to many people; sometimes it even seems improbable to me. But, tell me, is there another town with the energy and verve and sophistication of the Big Apple? I've toured —and enjoyed—great cities around the world, and I've come to believe that New York is simply one of a kind.

This is Central Park South at Sixth Avenue, a corner that typifies the ebullience and energy that is New York at its best. I've tried to capture the motion of the street in this canvas, one of my earliest efforts depicting a city setting. I also had fun painting the hansom cabs that are, to this day, one of the great traditions of Central Park.

At its best, New York is a place of great optimism, of new beginnings. I hope this captures a bit of that optimistic energy on canvas.

*Oil on canvas, 30"x 24"*

# NEW YORK
## *Snow on Seventh Avenue, 1932*

For the most part, I paint places I can see and experience first hand, though occasionally I enjoy the challenge of creating a romantic vision of another era. Seventh Avenue in New York in the 20's and early 30's was a bustling center of activity. The Pennsylvania Hotel, seen at the right of my painting, was the largest hotel in the world when completed in 1919. Across the street, the neo-classic entrance to the famous Pennsylvania Station (opened in 1910) buzzes with people preparing for departure.

To set the mood in the painting, I included many vintage vehicles, among them a Ford five window coupe, a Cadillac V-16 touring car, an early checkered cab and a few Seventh Avenue trollies. Signage and billboards are mostly period, though I frequently fabricate signs just for the fun of it. For example, the billboard to the immediate left of the Pennsylvania hotel proudly announces the virtues of "Church Brand Cleaner" with an image of an erupting volcano as a background. This sign was invented for fun: a tribute to a great painting by one of my favorite nineteenth century painters, Frederick Church.

*Oil on canvas, 24" x 30"*

# Paris, City of Lights

## Le Boulevard des Lumiere, at Dusk

My love affair with Paris started when I was a struggling young painter. You see, one of my first patrons maintained a caravan (or motor home as we call it) in Europe and I traded him a painting for its use for six weeks one spring. Nanette and I drove it into Paris and actually lived on the streets of the "City of Lights" for a blissful five days while I painted away to my heart's content.

Since then, Paris has been a romantic favorite. Broad boulevards, flower vendors, sidewalk cafes, and the ceaseless bustle of cars and people; it's all part of the charm of one of the world's most cosmopolitan cities. I found it a great pleasure just sitting in the cafes at night, nursing a cappuccino and watching the pageant of Parisian life pass by.

"Paris, City of Lights" could be titled "The Kinkade family in Paris." I've set the time machine back a few decades and included myself (in the red beret), painting the fabulous Cafe Nanette (named after my wife). The real Nanette, holding baby Chandler, hails a cab, while our oldest daughter Merritt looks on. I've even signed the tiny canvas on the street artist's easel — to my knowledge the smallest Kinkade signature on record! And in true Kinkade tradition, fifteen hidden "N"s grace the painting as a tribute to my Parisian belle, Nanette.

*Oil on canvas, 20"x 30"*

# DAWSON

## The Yukon River with Gold Seekers
## Landing by Moonlight in 1898

"Dawson" returns me to the beginnings of my career as an artist. Along with "Placerville, 1916", it was my first offering to the print collecting public. This exciting subject also brings me back to one of my most grand artistic adventures. Some years ago, I packed my paints and took a two week sketching tour through the far reaches of the Alaskan wilderness.

It was often so cold that the water colors I was using simply froze; I finally solved that problem by mixing the colors in rubbing alcohol instead of water. I'm grateful for that inspiration; it allowed me to create some canvases that, upon my return, expressed the intense isolation and fragile beauty of that remote, frozen region.

This work depicts the famous Yukon town of Dawson during the height of the northern gold rush, around 1898. We see gold seekers arriving in the primitive, crudely made, boats with which they navigated the Yukon River. Even with today's technology, surviving in extreme conditions is a challenge. The era I depicted in "Dawson" must have been brutal indeed. Yet, with the hardships of survival, comes the exuberance of comraderie. I hope I've captured both aspects in this work, one of the most detailed of my early career.

*Oil on canvas, 24"x 36"*

# PLACERVILLE
## Main Street at Dusk, 1916

This is a great personal favorite of mine; one of the two prints that actually launched my career as a published artist and one of the rarest of all Thomas Kinkade prints.

It fascinates me now that I chose this nostalgic view of my home town as the subject for the work of art that's played such an important part in my own personal history. I was intrigued by the idea that sleepy little Placerville has a history, that its streets were once filled with what we now see as vintage cars in the decade when it, and America, were awakening to the Twentieth Century.

As it turns out, Thomas Kinkade art also has a history.

And "Placerville, 1916" has come to represent much the same thing in my own body of work as the subject it depicts—a simpler past, viewed now in the warm light of nostalgic memory.

By the way, for those who might want to see this original painting, it was installed in 1984 as a permanent exhibit in the central room of the El Dorado County Main Library in Placerville. If you ever pass through the area, please feel free to stop by for a peek. And if you're so inclined, visit the historic main street of Placerville and see how much the town has changed since 1916!

*Oil on canvas, 36"x 60"*

# SAN FRANCISCO

## *Market Street and the Ferry Building, at Dusk, 1909*

The heart of San Francisco is the bay, with its wharves and myriad fishing boats, its bustle of activity in the morning and again in the evening, when the fleet returns laden with fish.

That's true today and it was ever so much more true in 1909, when the sea provided a bountiful harvest. There's the promise of adventure in the very smell of the briny air; at the turn of the century the bay was alive with seafaring men of every description—colorful characters who spoke exotic languages and told marvelous tales.

The voyages that began and ended at the old ferry building were of a somewhat more modest character and yet, not without their own romance. Ferries plied the bay, connecting San Francisco with the many quaint villages along the shore. In "San Francisco, Market Street" we visit a time when auto travel was less than convenient, and the ferries that came and went from the old building at the foot of Market Street provided the most practical transport to the bustling bay area towns.

Practical, and yet, oh so romantic. With its cable cars and ferries, San Francisco has always been a city where travel is a charming adventure.

*Oil on canvas, 30"x 48"*

# Old Sacramento

This painting was originally commissioned by a retired California politician who wanted to share some of the charm of the capital city with others. It has since come to be a very popular print that for most people has very little to do with the specific location it portrays. I think the reason for this is clear; we all like a celebration.

"Old Sacramento" depicts a celebration that could occur on any holiday in any city in America. The mood is joyous.

The activities are plentiful. The energy is contagious. I especially like many of the hidden details in this piece. The fluffy dog is a portrait of a friend's family pet. Many of the models for the people were family members or friends. Even the signs have special meanings; the "Grady's Fajitas" sign barely visible on the ground floor of the main building to the left is a tribute to an old friend whose cooking is legendary!

*Oil on canvas, 24"x 36"*

# SAN FRANCISCO
## Late Afternoon at Union Square

As a young boy my first glimpse of San Francisco came during a sightseeing trip with my brother and father. Upon passing over the Bay Bridge and being awestruck by the mysterious beauty of the lights reflecting on the bay, my father turned to me and said, "Now you know why they call it *The City*." Since that moment, San Francisco has always remained The City in my heart.

In "San Francisco, Late Afternoon at Union Square" I wanted to capture the lights and motion that are the essence of San Francisco. I chose the view looking uphill on Powell Street to emphasize the sense of distant activity. Since the Powell Street line is one of the most popular cable car routes, I naturally included a heavily loaded example making its way to Fisherman's Wharf.

As well as fine shops and hotels, Union Square is home to many art galleries. As a student at nearby U. C. Berkeley in the mid-seventies, my artistic direction was shaped by the great landscape paintings on display in these galleries. Since we visit Union Square so often, I included a cameo portrait of my wife, daughter Merritt, and myself in the lower right hand corner as joyful observers of the busy scene.

*Oil on canvas, 36"x 30"*

# Christmas at the Courthouse

Perhaps the Christmas present I'd like most would be a time machine. I seem to have a powerful urge to celebrate this wonderful holiday with my great grandparents or perhaps even with Charles Dickens in Victorian London.

"Christmas at the Courthouse" displays the nostalgic charm I find in the spirited Christmas celebrations of a more innocent era. The street, crowded with shoppers and celebrants, and lined with wonderful vintage cars, is as festive as a brilliantly lit Christmas tree. There is a joy to the bustling crowds, and a warm comraderie among the friends who stop on the street to talk and share holiday plans. Snow transforms the familiar courthouse and town center into something wondrous and strange. It is nature's Christmas decoration; I can hardly imagine the holiday season without the festive addition of snow.

In a way, I do have a time machine —my art. Paintings like "Christmas at the Courthouse" let me create—and then enjoy— rich, imaginative worlds that preserve the very best of the past.

*Oil on canvas, 24"x 36"*

# SAN FRANCISCO
## A View Down California Street From Nob Hill

I was recently talking to a friend who had relocated near San Francisco and who had never before been to that city. I was trying to summarize my various feelings about one of my favorite cities and found words completely inadequate to explain the sensations that grip me when I'm in San Francisco. Perhaps that's why I'm an artist. The lights, the mood, the flying flags and windswept wisps of fog, the bustling people and quaint bits of architecture that are San Francisco can perhaps best be captured on canvas. Yet even this is inadequate, for a purely visual image cannot relate the ambient sounds and smells that are so much a part of the "City By The Bay". For example, if you were standing at the location I painted, your ears would probably be filled with the sounds of clanging cable car bells, the whistle of hotel bellmen flagging taxis, and perhaps the lonely call of seagulls overhead. Likewise, if you took a deep breath you might notice the aroma of fried rice rising from Chinatown below, or perhaps the pungent smell of sourdough bread that seems at times to be omnipresent in San Francisco. But before I ramble on too much, perhaps I better just make plans to get back to San Francisco for another visit!

*Oil on canvas, 24"x 20"*

# Thomas Kinkade's
## Cottages of Light

Though I don't usually paint people, I do paint portraits. Portraits of the quiet dignity of honest, simple folk as reflected in honest, simple homes: the cottages or village houses of another era. I like to think of homes as pieces of living history—silently documenting the struggles and triumphs of their inhabitants.

I'm fascinated by the places in which people live and particularly by the humble cottages that have provided shelter to family after family, often for hundreds of years. Every detail of their appearance—their carefully thatched roofs, their painted shutters, the way the wood or stone has weathered, the furnishings glimpsed through windows, the flagstone walks, the bowers and gardens that surround them—all bespeak the creative human effort and the peaceful serenity of a life lived close to the land.

These cottages remind us of the things that people value most. In an important sense, each one is a revealing portrait of the family that has lived within its walls and called it home. My "Cottages of Light" are often something else as well. They can be romantic embodiments of our hopes and dreams, ideal expressions of our fondest sentiments and aspirations. Some of these cottages are my dream-visions of a perfect weekend hideaway with my wife, Nanette. Some may be an ideal vacation spot, or the ultimate mountain retreat, or perhaps a dream home with an ocean view. I've lived in each one—at least in my imagination. And there's room in each cottage for you, as well. Come on in, the tea is brewing!

# Chandler's Cottage

Cottages have personalities. I firmly believe that, and I've lately discovered that I share my belief with some very surprising, and surprisingly wise, little people; my own beautiful daughters, Merritt and Chandler.

I love to watch my girls at play—their energy and humor and surprising insights are an endless source of amusement. They love their doll houses, love to decorate them in the most fanciful manner. They treat the houses like little playmates, friends with very definite personalities. Lately, in my travels, I've been on the lookout for cottages that would make perfect dream dollhouses for my girls. How little Chandler would love to have a real miniature version of this delightful, flower-bedecked hutch complete with blooming garden, in her playroom. Like most little girls, she loves fancy, frilly things and this hidden little house seems to be a confection of gingerbread and spun sugar.

I originally created "Chandler's Cottage" and its companion piece, "Merritt's Cottage" as tributes to my two girls. I suppose the special love I lavished on these paintings has born some special fruit, for both have been enormously popular. Perhaps other proud parents can see their daughter's dreams inside the walls of these special places as well.

*Oil on canvas, 16"x 20"*

# Cottage by the Sea

Recently while visiting the Pacific coast of northern California, I was browsing through a colorful real estate booklet. I kept noticing the phrase "Ocean View" highlighted in the ads. What I found interesting was that most of the photos of houses accompanying this description seemed to have little, if any, view of the ocean. I began to daydream about my romantic associations with the ocean—days spent wandering the rugged coast of California, walking hand in hand with my wife, Nanette. I imagined a coastal residence that would be my ideal seaside cottage—the kind not usually found in real estate booklets!

Though this cottage doesn't exist anywhere but in my painting, I think for many of us it represents a dream seaside getaway. Here you could spend quiet evenings by the fire while the surf crashes rhythmically outside. When the tide is out, you could wander amongst the rocks searching for the perfect seashell for your collection while the lonely call of seagulls echoes overhead. Of course, I had to paint the scene at sunset. After all, what would a seaside cottage be without a beautiful sunset to watch?

By the way, as I worked on this painting, I envisioned an aged captain living in the cottage. I hung a brass ship's bell atop the lightpost in front of the cottage with red and green signal lights below it; the same kind of lights used to hang on the twin smokestacks of Mississippi riverboats as a signal in the night to other boats. When the green light was on the left, you knew the riverboat was coming towards you and vice versa. But though the color of the lights might in this context be purely decorative, for this retired captain the bell atop has a very practical purpose: two sharp rings send the signal, "Prepare for visitors to come aboard!"

*Oil on canvas, 20" x 30"*

# Evening at Merritt's Cottage

My daughter Merritt loves sunsets. So of course, when on the lookout for Merritt's dream cottage, I paid particular attention to sunset. The house should come alive in the warm glow of dusk, just the way my older daughter does.

"Evening at Merritt's Cottage" is exactly what I was looking for—and Merritt certainly agrees. The cottage glimmers most invitingly in the pink-purple evening light; it seems almost to smile its welcome. My little Merritt is very neat and tidy, delicate and ladylike. She loves to entertain her girlfriends at prim and proper doll teas, and she'd be delighted if her daddy's friends could drop in for dessert and share an "Evening at Merritt's Cottage." I'm sure the painting has had a strong effect on her little imagination. After all, it's the only print of daddy's work that hangs in her room. In fact, it's given a place of honor—right above her bed.

*Oil on canvas, 16"x 20"*

# Glory of Morning

*I* like to think that one thing that separates artists from most people is that we're alive to the world around us; we take delight in things many people never even notice. Delight—the word itself intrigues me because "light" is such an important part of it. For me the quality of light is a delight! The play of light and shadow on a day dappled with clouds, the way sunlight teases nature's colors into life—these are my great artistic challenges.

Twice each day nature puts on a light show of wonderful subtlety. Morning light is warm with the energy of a new day, yet cool with the moisture of mist. My "Glory of Morning" sparkles with the light of just such a morning—warm light filtered through myriads of tiny water drops until the colors glisten.

You can see that light reflected on the flowers of a fabulous garden. Each color is so vibrant that the garden becomes a living rainbow. Flowers are alive to the quality of light. Spend a day in a garden—watch it change as the light changes—and you'll see what I mean; "Glory of Morning" celebrates the "wake up call" for nature's colors.

*Oil on canvas, 8"x 10"*

# Glory of Evening

It may seem that sunset is the mirror image of sunrise, but a painter who pays close attention to visual detail, knows that isn't so. I painted "Glory of Evening" as a companion piece to "Glory of Morning" and yet each is unique.

I'm fascinated by the subtleties of transitional light— the interludes between dark and day when the sky flames with a special radiance, when colors are heightened and shadows dance on the ground.

"Glory of Evening" was created to be as distinctive as a sunset where the dust of a busy day and low lying clouds reflect the violet rays of the sun. The cozy thatched roof cottage answers the glow of dusk with its own warm radiance, providing safe haven against the advancing dark. It's a new addition to the fabulous imaginary village of perfect little homes that grows only on this artist's canvas. As the sun moves to meet the horizon, its lavender radiance colors the garden flowers, deepening their hues. Such glorious evenings as this lay a regal purple cloak upon the land— and every home becomes a castle.

*Oil on canvas, 8"x 10"*

JOHN 3:16

# The Hidden Cottage

How many of us get to come face to face with our fantasies about fabulous, joyous places that are simply more special than our everyday world? It happened to me, especially in England, where so many rural paths seem to lead to utterly charming, half-hidden cottages like this one; where rustic gates open onto romantic hideaways.

The English countryside is rich with human history; even the gardens and cobbled paths have a "lived in" look.

The very stones are worn by the touch of human hands; lives have been lived and romantic dramas played out within these walls. Even the soft, luminous atmosphere, heavy with fog and mist, is richly nostalgic.

"The Hidden Cottage" is a treasure composed in equal measure of dreams and memories. Once discovered and painted it is a treasure for all to share.

*Oil on canvas, 16" x 20"*

# The Hidden Cottage II

*I* take great pleasure in finding out-of-the-way places, small wonders that sometimes seem to go unnoticed until they're transformed into works of art like "Hidden Cottage II." I discovered this inspiration in the town of Carmel-by-the-Sea where there are lovely little cottages bathed in my favorite light—strong, oblique rays of sun that paint long, feathery shadows on the ground as they pass through the slats of antique wooden gates.

I'm not really sure whether it's the act of exploration, or the charming cottage that crowns it, that pleases me most. I firmly believe that the world rewards the bold and curious with exciting discoveries—and the "Hidden Cottage" series bears this out.

Great cottages like this are built by people who understand the urge to explore. The cottages are always half-hidden behind hedges, fences, at the far end of long gardens. That's why I like them so.

*Oil on canvas, 16"x 12"*

# Julianne's Cottage

Often, researching subjects can be such a serendipity of circumstances that I can only thank God for His divine guidance! This painting is a good example of this. While visiting England one fall, my wife and I decided to take a driving trip to the lake district—a beautiful area of England known for its spectacular scenery as well as the home of Beatrix Potter, the famous creator of Peter Rabbit and other stories. While we made our way north, we thumbed through some tourist guides and found the names of one or two bed and breakfasts where we could set up shop for a few days as I worked on a lake district painting.

On arriving in the area, we soon discovered that not only were all of our choices of lodging completely booked, but virtually everything else we could find was full as well! With hungry, tired children in the back seat, we said a quick prayer and drove on, searching for some place, any place, to put up for the night. While heading down an obscure country road, we passed several large farms, one of which had a tiny, almost unnoticeable sign out front that said simply: "B & B." Not only did this farm have a comfortable room available for the night, but it turned out to be a farm originally owned by none other than Beatrix Potter herself! I quickly set to work the next morning, surrounded by the sounds of sheep, geese, and other farm creatures, and the result is the painting I call "Julianne's Cottage." By the way, our room during our stay was the one in the upper left-hand corner of the cottage!

*Oil on canvas, 12"x 16"*

# LAMPLIGHT LANE
## The Brooke Windermer and Cottage Row at Dusk

An artist's imagination is affected by both his inner thoughts and his surrounding world. "Lamplight Lane" shows just what I mean.

Talk about an idyllic spot: quaint English cottages running along a footpath, a lively stream spanned by an ornate Victorian bridge, sunlight breaking through clouds. It's all so perfect that I must have dreamed it up, right? Not at all. Actually, I painted "Lamplight Lane" almost completely on location, at a charming little village in the English Cotswolds that looked very much like this image. My imagination supplied only the finishing details. To heighten the romance I added lampposts running along the brook like a string of luminous pearls. For drama, I supplied golden beams breaking through the clouds so that it seems the floor of heaven has cracked open and God's own light is pouring out.

I hold "Lamplight Lane" very dear. In fact, I gave the original to my wife as a housewarming gift for our new home. My hope is that it may grace your home with warmth and joy as well.

*Oil on canvas, 12"x 16"*

# The Lit Path

If a cottage reflects on its owner, then judging from the profusion of lights surrounding this cottage, the owner must be very cheery indeed. Lights are always a favorite subject of mine, especially when they seem to beckon me towards a cozy setting. The lights along this walkway not only beckon, they light the way, which is especially needful for steps that in typical English fashion seem as irregular as the ground they traverse.

The thatching on this cottage is also of note, being that lovely grayish tone that denotes age. It seems that thatch, which consists of straw or reeds, has a golden amber color when first applied, but mellows with age into a cool gray appearance. The owners of this cottage seem truly sensible. Not only have they provided a glowing footpath for visitors, but they appear in no hurry to replace the thatch. This makes fine fiscal sense to my mind; with a life expectancy for thatching that can reach as high as 75 years, perhaps it's just as well to let the grandchildren re-thatch the roof!

*Oil on canvas, 8"x 10"*

# Olde Porterfield Gift Shoppe

Snowfall is like morning mist at the ocean; it silently shrouds the landscape and creates a nostalgic, dreamy mood. I love the hush that snowfall brings, as though the whole world has taken a deep breath in anticipation and is quietly awaiting some magical moment.

As an artist, I face the challenge of painting falling snow in such a way that suggests the gentle movement of the flakes throwing the world into a subtle blur. It's also necessary to portray the depth of the falling flakes, with larger snowflakes in the foreground and smaller ones receding into the distance. Lastly, I always try to avoid being too monochromatic in my palette with snow scenes. There's a tremendous amount of color in even the most subtle of settings. In this case, I tried to suggest the different tones of the sky as contrasted to the subtle grays and mauves of the foreground snow. I also enjoyed the effect of light cascading from the windows onto the snow below as though an illuminated welcome mat were inviting passersby to inspect the wares of the gift shoppe.

*Oil on canvas, 16"x 20"*

# Mc Kenna's Cottage

There seems to be a quiet stateliness to classic English cottages. Everything about them seems timeless and enduring. Every stone seems placed by hand, every bit of thatch carefully bound in place. No hydraulic tools are used to create a cottage—no electric saws or bulldozers; this is a patient labor of love.

I am reminded of these somewhat elusive characteristics when I see the painting "McKenna's Cottage." This piece was executed almost entirely on location as I watched evening approach over this lovely thatched cottage. As I painted, an elderly gentleman with a wheelbarrow was painstakingly repairing a portion of the stone wall in the foreground. I was struck by the man's silent diligence. The thought occurred to me that the scene I was watching could just as easily have been taking place a hundred years ago.

Though I never discovered the name of this cottage I named it "McKenna's Cottage" as a tribute to "McKenna", the toddler daughter of a good friend who purchased the original painting.

*Oil on canvas, 12"x 16"*

# The Miller's Cottage, Thomashire

During my recent stay in the Cotswold district of England, I was struck by the simple and measured routine of daily life. Rituals and habits are not built around cars and freeways, but around the plodding pace of foot travel and village life. "The Miller's Cottage" is a tribute to one of the most pervasive of English village rituals: feeding the ducks at the local mill pond. As I sat observing the tranquil scene, I was amazed at how many people would visit the pond to throw stale bread and biscuits to the ducks and geese. Indeed, at certain times of the day I would observe entire lines of young mothers pushing baby carriages (prams as the English call them) waiting their turn to toss bread. I'm sure the ducks at that pond are amongst the best fed in England!

By the way, the water warden who looks after the pond lives in this quaint cottage, which actually was once a functioning mill. The water runs down these waterfalls, or raceways, which travel under the stone cottage and originally turned a large waterwheel inside the mill. Though the water wheel is gone, the waterfalls added a pleasant sound as I sat in the sunshine working on this painting. Over the weeks I was at work, I too got in the habit of feeding the ducks. In time, the more adventurous of these would regularly settle themselves in the shade beneath my easel!

*Oil on canvas, 12"x 16"*

# Olde Porterfield Tea Room

It seems that every time I visit England, another new aspect begins to enchant me. On my most recent visit, my wife and I were completely taken with the traditions of English tea. It became almost as though we were on a search to find the finest serving of High Tea in the land. As we travelled about, each village where we would stop to paint would provide another opportunity for sampling the local tea rooms. Our favorite places served what is called "Creamed Teas," so named for the rich local cream that accompanied the steaming pots of tea.

"Olde Porterfield Tea Room," though imaginary, is based on those wonderful tea rooms that along with pubs seem to be the social center of every English country village. In this case, the tea room is fashioned from what was originally a cottage. As is so often the case in England, this cottage features architecture that is an amalgamation of every addition and alteration that came through the successive generations. Though one occupant preferred stone construction, another might prefer brick windows; dormers and extra rooms were added as needed. No general plan was necessary—you simply changed what was there to suit your needs. Though this kind of construction may seem haphazard to an American, the end result is, simply put, charming.

*Oil on canvas, 16"x 20"*

# Open Gate, Sussex

Open gates are an invitation to visit, especially when lights glow warmly within an English cottage. If you're in the mood to chat, you might wander up the rutted lane and knock briskly on the old, weather-worn door. If your neighbor is home, you will soon be sitting beside the hearth with a warm cup of tea, sweetened lightly with fresh cream.

On a chilly October evening my wife, Nanette, and I were invited inside a charming cottage similar to the one depicted in "Open Gate, Sussex." The elderly couple who owned the cottage had been so excited by the painting I was working on in the lane outside their home that they had immediately extended an invitation to "come inside for a warm-up." The toasty kitchen just inside the door was aglow from the fire in a small fireplace and the ample windows looked out over a garden that even in October was radiant with color. Even geese couldn't resist visiting such a delightful spot!

*Oil on canvas, 8"x 10"*

# The Rose Arbor Cottage

It seems that flowers have a kind of flair for the dramatic. What I mean is this: whenever I discover a soaring cliff, a hidden waterfall, a rushing brook, it will inevitably be festooned with wildflowers. It's as if the flowers sought out settings of extraordinary beauty and drama.

That's certainly true of the lush roses in "Rose Arbor Cottage." They blossom before a lovely, half-hidden cottage— a secluded and most romantic spot. If roses are the emblems of love, then they have designated this as an ideal hideaway for young lovers. The enigmatic young lady who stands alone and expectant beneath the rose arbor is surely a featured player in a romantic play of some sort. It may be that she has planned a rendezvous with her beau at this precise spot; or, perhaps, she merely pauses here before meeting her beloved within. Perhaps she is herself an artist, and like me, is entranced with the timeless beauty of an arbor in bloom.

*Oil on canvas, 16"x 20"*

# Evening at Swanbrooke Cottage, Thomashire

In England, walking trails accompany even the smallest stream and on a summer's evening, a peaceful stroll beside a gently whispering brook is guaranteed to restore even the most burdened soul. On one such evening walk in England, my family and I came upon the cottage on which I based this painting. The brook-side walking trail led invitingly to the doorstep of the cottage, almost as though a welcome were being extended. The next week I set up my easel on the bank of the brook opposite the cottage and for several days worked on this painting with the sound of the brook in my ears.

I began to imagine myself living in this idyllic cottage, with the entrancing sound of the tiny brook as a constant back-drop to a peaceful life. I was intrigued by the simplicity of the life of the cottage's inhabitants, with patient gardening and a daily ritual of feeding ducks and swans taking center stage in their existence. I hope "Evening at Swanbrooke Cottage" captures on canvas a bit of the peacefulness of such a life, for I'm sure each of us has at times daydreamed of living beside a lush and beautiful stream.

*Oil on canvas, 20"x 24"*

# Weathervane Hutch

Behind the overgrown garden walls of the studio I used while visiting the Cotswold region of England, was the hidden pathway leading to "Weathervane Hutch." I discovered it by accident one day, when searching for a shortcut to the village square. From the moment I saw its flower draped facade, I knew I would paint it some day. As one might expect, this tiny cottage was inhabited by an absolutely charming elderly woman who, in her very British way, gave me a brief history of the little cottage. She gave me permission to set up my easel in the narrow drive that led to her cottage, and a few days later I began work.

Like many of the paintings from my last stay in England, this piece was executed almost entirely outdoors, directly from the subject. As I scrutinized the details of the small house, I became enchanted with the weathervane atop the slate roof, which was so detailed as to almost appear to be a small sculpture. The weathervane depicts a plowman working behind a large draft horse in the manner common to rural farms of this region in the era before steam power became the norm. Though in my painting this detail is only a fraction of an inch in size, the weathervane is the cornerstone of the small cottage and I couldn't resist including it in the title. By the way, the word "hutch" is often used in England to refer to cottages which are especially tiny, though to American ears the word probably sounds more like a piece of furniture.

*Oil on canvas, 8"x 10"*

# HEATHER'S HUTCH
## Sugar and Spice Cottages I

*I* have just the prescription for anyone who's feeling cynical or flippant or world-weary: *Daughters!*

The playful high-spirits and sense of wonder that my little girls, Merritt and Chandler, bring to my world inspire and invigorate me. What imaginations they have! They'll notice one tiny detail in a painting and weave a whole story from it.

I've paid tribute to the "everything nice" world of little girls before, but my new Sugar and Spice Cottages is the first series solely devoted to "dollhouse" cottages that my little girls would love to live in. "Heather's Hutch", which leads off the series, is no dollhouse—it's inspired by a real stone cottage I discovered in the English Cotswolds. But the thatched roof and pink and white dogwoods make it especially attractive to young ladies and I just know there's a little play garden behind the gate.

The hen with her chicks and pigeons are for my little Chandler, who gets so excited whenever she sees birds. And the rich plum color on the doors above the windows is for another favorite "girl" of mine—my lovely wife, Nanette.

*Oil on canvas, 8"x 10"*

# THOMAS KINKADE'S
## Seasons of Light

*T*here is a majesty, and great comfort, in the procession of the seasons. As a poet once said, "If winter's come, can spring be far behind?" There is, also, a temptation to organize our lives in terms of months and years, and to overlook the very distinctive pleasures of the seasons.

In a sense, a painted image exists outside of time—it is a moment made eternal. For that reason, as an artist, I feel drawn to direct our attention away from the passing of time and to focus my work on the timeless qualities of special moments: the fleeting emotions brought by such things as sunsets and morning mist and the smell of burning leaves. These romantic, indefinable sensations that we all feel at times are the subject of my paintings. That's why I like the changing of the seasons so much. Seasons are spring boards for these timeless moments. Each one is a state of being,

with its distinctive themes, rhythms, moods and emotions. That profound truth is the great discovery of these paintings and, I hope, what will be communicated to others.

My "Seasons of Light" are never simple studies of a particular place viewed casually at a certain time of year. Each one is, instead, an attempt to evoke the special character of the season; to connect it to emotions and experiences that make it distinctive, vital, and urgently important to me. The energy and vibrant optimism of Spring, the vitality and accomplishment of Summer, the ripeness and fulfillment of Autumn, the contemplative calm of Winter—these are the real subjects of my "Seasons of Light." Breath deep—Fall is in the air. Or could it be the gentle fragrance of Spring?

# AMBER AFTERNOON
## Burning Leaves on a Quiet Saturday

Longfellow's admonition to "... stay at home, my heart and rest ..." is easy for me to understand on an autumn day. The gathering breezes carry leaves to the ground, while all around, the crimson shroud of color creates a glow that warms the soul. I enjoy putting on sweaters for the first time in months and building that first fire of the season in the fireplace. Above all, I look forward to the scent of autumn; the cooling moisture of rains and mist and the occasional scent of burning leaves.

It's time to set aside the yearnings and adventures of summer and turn our hearts to home and rest.

This painting is a poem for fall—a romantic love sonnet from the heart of one who feels deeply the charms of the autumnal season. I chose the subtle colors of a vintage Victorian house as a means of accentuating the brilliant fall color, and of course, I had to include the smoldering pile of leaves.

*Oil on canvas, 16" x 20"*

# THE VILLAGE INN
## Country Memories II

Nanette and I fell in love with the "bed and breakfast" during our travels in England—where a B & B sign outside a home (its only advertising) promises comfortable lodging, good company, and a hearty morning meal. If you want to learn about a place and its people, stop at a B & B. There's no substitute.

That's why we're so delighted to see charming country inns popping up in our country as well. "The Village Inn" features climbing blue wisteria and ornate white wrought iron furniture that invites you to enjoy the verdant lawn. I softened the focus just a little, and heightened the romance of a very romantic setting to make this B & B my dream-vision of an intimate, utterly charming bed and breakfast.

High-rise hotels can be quite comfortable, but Nanette and I prefer the charm of a quiet "bed & breakfast" where we feel more "at home." I hope this country inn will make others feel "at home" as well.

*Oil on canvas, 12"x 16"*

# Blossom Hill Church

Country churches seem to nestle into their surroundings like a small child on his mother's lap. I've often noted how natural a church can seem as it sits amidst the landscape. It seems such an organic part of its environment—almost as though without it, something would be missing. "Blossom Hill Church" the second piece in my "Country Church Collection," is especially fused with its setting; immersed within the enchanting web of spring's full bloom. If I seem particularly romantic about this church, I am. For me, "Blossom Hill Church" will always exist in a world of spring and flowers. After all, inside this church on a brilliant spring morning in 1982, my wife Nanette and I were married. Interestingly enough, for many years we and our two children made our home less than five miles from this historic and magical setting.

Speaking of two children, please notice the small placard along the pathway indicating the resident minister. Its words, "Rev. Merritt Chandler" are a tribute to my two daughters, Merritt and Chandler. My trademark "N", signifying my wife Nanette, adorns the doorway.

As dusk settles on "Blossom Hill Church", the evening service is at hand. The glowing lights tell of worshippers inside, perhaps praising God in a joyful chorus. As a man who deeply values his Christian faith, I cherish the sense of warmth and hope engendered by this illuminated church. I hope this painting will share this hope with others. After all, men build buildings, but only God's love can build a church.

*Oil on canvas, 24"x 30"*

# Spring at Stonegate

Some contrasts are wonderfully suggestive to the artist: light breaking through clouds, ice melting into a rushing stream, a flower growing in rocks. The brilliant contrasting with the subtle, the permanent with the transitory, these things provide some of my richest subjects.

While strolling with my wife through the English countryside, I happened upon this magnificent stone cottage, nestled amongst greening trees and a lavish garden. The stone itself was massive, weathered, impervious to changes of climate or season.

But the blooming world around was exquisitely sensitive to every cloudburst, every soft breeze, every golden shower of sunshine.

The contrast between stone and flower, between the obdurate rock and the sensitive plant, the enduring and the evanescent is at the heart of "Spring at Stonegate." To our delight, the living world re-awakens each year at the touch of a spring breeze. But it is also a comfort to know that Stonegate itself will endure, unchanged, through all the changing weathers.

*Oil on canvas, 12"x 16"*

# The Ice Harvest

There's something festive about even the hard work of winter. Maybe it's the colorful, heavy clothing of the season. Or the fires, needed for warmth, that flicker merrily, casting shadows. Perhaps, as in "The Ice Harvest", it's the bustling activity of the groups of people who gather to accomplish the season's tasks, and to celebrate its holidays. Certainly the snow always adds a nostalgic touch.

Harvesting ice was one of the great communal activities that gave village life at the turn of the century its character and closeness. During the sparseness of winter, ice was a giant cash crop for farmers in northern regions, and like the autumnal harvests of grain and vegetables, it brought people together in a common cause. The draught horses are wonderful, muscular beasts who snort steaming clouds of breath into the air. Their sleds are piled high with ice and hauled to the thick-walled stone storage house, where the blocks will remain frozen throughout the year, to be sent to buyers from the great hotels and restaurants of nearby cities.

The whole scene is bathed in a golden glow that floods out of the windows of the ice house office—a reflection of the high spirits and good fellowship that warm the scene.

*Oil on canvas, 24"x 36"*

# BEYOND AUTUMN GATE
## Morning at Ivycrest Manor

Some years ago during my travels through England, I found a wonderful old stone gate—mysterious and inviting, suggesting all sorts of exciting possibilities. It was only when I was back in my studio, working on the canvas that would become my well known "Autumn Gate", that I realized I didn't know where the gate led. Was it the entrance to a glorious castle or simply a country road leading to some less picturesque setting? When people asked, I wasn't able to answer because I'd never walked in to take a look.

This question intrigued me to such a degree that on a later trip, Nanette and I made a pilgrimage back to the setting for "Autumn Gate." Walking through it, I was ecstatic to discover the stately, ivy draped stone manor house I celebrate in this painting. Since this subject lay beyond the gate featured in "Autumn Gate", I couldn't resist titling it "Beyond Autumn Gate."

Setting aside the history of its inspiration, I also wanted to create a splendid evocation of a home more gracious than the humble cottages I often paint. I'm sure deep down, each of us dreams of living in a setting such as this and being, if only in our imagination, "Lord of the Manor."

*Oil on canvas, 24"x 30"*

# Sunday at Apple Hill

Perhaps for as long as there have been Sunday afternoons there have been Sunday afternoon drives. In the spring, I enjoy packing up the family after our Sunday worship at church and wandering about in search of wildflowers and picnic spots. Though the carriage we wander about in is of the horseless variety, I sometimes envy the days when the family outing to church meant sitting aboard a buggy and slowly touring the countryside. It seems the slower pace of horse-drawn travel makes for a greater appreciation of the beauty of the scenery. Also, there is something magical about being surrounded by the sounds and smells of the countryside as you travel in an open air buggy. A fragrant field of flowers seems to explode with life as the air carries the fragrance to the passer-by and the songs of birds on a sunny afternoon would lift any spirit.

The house featured in "Sunday at Apple Hill" is a vintage farm house which is actually located in an area near my home known as Apple Hill. Though the setting is based on this lovely old house, I enhanced the flowers and foliage surrounding it a bit to add color to the painting. And, of course, I couldn't resist adding the family returning from church as a tribute to the slower-paced life of yesteryear.

*Oil on canvas, 20"x 24"*

# Moonlit Sleigh Ride

A few years back I had a marvelous experience of cross-country skiing through a snowy valley by moonlight. I'll never forget the impression that the adventure made on me. Moonlight on snow is a beautiful sight—a combination of subtle, luminous light areas, and dark, mysterious shadows. My imagination was filled with visions of homesteaders making their way home through the snow by the light of the moon. I was especially struck by the cozy sight of our forest cabin as we concluded our moonlit ski trip. The warm, inviting glow of the tiny hut threw patches of radiant light on the surrounding snowbanks. This painting is a tribute to that romantic evening, with the exception of the skis; instead, a nostalgic sleigh whisks through the moonlit forest. What could be nicer than returning to the inviting glow of a warm fireside after a frosty evening sleigh ride?

*Oil on canvas, 8"x 10"*

# Sweetheart Cottage

To paraphrase Jerome, "Love is a pure light that ignites the cozy fire of affection." If ever a cozy fire of affection burned brightly, it is within the weathered stone walls of "Sweetheart Cottage." Perhaps my sentimental Irish nature is shining through, but I happen to be enchanted with the idea of a romantic hideaway hidden amidst blossoming flowers. "Sweetheart Cottage" is my first attempt to put on canvas this dreamy notion, and it comes at a time especially meaningful to me. In 1992 my wife Nanette and I celebrated our tenth year of marriage. Actually, this painting is sort of a dual tribute. Not only does it commemorate our tenth wedding anniversary, but "Sweetheart Cottage" is also a salute to the most romantic occasion of the year, Valentine's Day. In fact, I have made "Sweetheart Cottage" an annual series which will debut around Valentine's Day each year, since I have many more "Romantic Hideaways" stored in my imagination.

For those who enjoy the hidden details that almost always appear in my paintings, this painting is a treasure trove! As a tribute to my wedding anniversary, the outdoor clock bears the time 5:02 (my anniversary is May 2nd) and the tiny picture, seen in the window to the left of the door, is a wedding portrait of Nanette and myself. The address placard says 214, this, along with the plentiful hearts, are references to Valentine's Day. And, of course, what would a Kinkade painting be without hidden "N"s as a momento for Nanette. This painting has seven of them so keep your magnifying glasses handy.

*Oil on canvas, 12" x 16"*

# Yosemite Valley
## Late Afternoon at Artist's Point

Nowhere on earth am I more aware of the sheer awesomeness of God's handiwork than Yosemite Valley. This painting depicts the valley as seen from a little known place called "Artist's Point", named in tribute to the many 19th century artists who favored it as a sketching ground. Thomas Hill, Albert Bierstadt and countless others painted this view long before I was even born and, perhaps challenged by their example, I decided to attempt painting the same vista.

The first difficulty is reaching the spot. A steep, poorly marked trail leads up the western escarpment of the valley and Artist's Point lies along that trail. Topographical maps help in the location process, but even with those, it's difficult to find because of the dense second growth. In my case, the hike was intensified by the 50 pounds or so of easel, paints and assorted other material strapped to my back!

The final result was worth the efforts however, because in 1989, the National Park System selected "Yosemite Valley" as their official print. This tribute was especially exciting since this piece was chosen out of about 2,700 other paintings created by many of America's top artists. In addition, "Yosemite Valley" was made into a commemorative stamp and gold medallion. I was thrilled with the honor, but after all, God alone deserves the credit for the beauty and majesty of Yosemite Valley.

*Oil on canvas, 18" x 24"*

# MOONLIT VILLAGE

## An Evening Service at the Church on the Hill, 1909

In my travels throughout America, I've noticed that churches are often built on a hillside or knoll as a means of emphasizing their presence in a town. I find this to be a particularly poignant concept. These hillside churches, like lighthouses, are high up, so that figuratively speaking their light might be seen from afar. I wanted to capture a bit of that feel in my painting, "Moonlit Village." To accentuate the beacon-like effect of the church, I chose a nocturnal composition which allowed me to illuminate the church from within. I also wanted to suggest the sense that the church was the social center of the village, so an evening service with villagers gathering from all directions was a natural composition. The snowy setting was chosen for no other reason than that I love the effect of moonlight on the snow with all the beautiful interplay of warm and cool colors.

Though the painting doesn't portray a particular town, I drew inspiration from towns in such divergent areas as Connecticut, North Carolina, Missouri and even Northern California. As a final romantic touch, I was inspired by my neighbor who places lit candles in small sand-filled paper bags to illuminate the way to his home at Christmas time. I included these glowing lights along the road in my painting, an appropriate touch since these candle bags were a tradition on festive winter evenings at the turn of the century.

*Oil on canvas, 36"x 30"*

# Sunday Outing
## Family Traditions I

Family traditions. They give us our uniqueness and character. And yet, because we're not really so different after all, they also affirm our common humanity.

A favorite Kinkade tradition is the Sunday drive. After church we'll take off in the family car, find a lovely, lazy back - road and see what treats it has in store. Often, we'll do our driving in California's Apple Hill country, where the neat orchards and charming old farm houses provide a comfortable reminder that families have been enjoying Sunday drives along these lanes since the horse-and-buggy days.

"Sunday Outing" presents just such a family. How proudly father drives his buggy from the carriage house; how festive wife and baby look; how excited brother and sister are. The morning itself is radiant with light warmed by a lingering dew. (Mornings like this have become an artistic tradition with me!)

At Apple Hill the past is not dry or distant. It lives again in our lives—and I find that thought very comforting.

*Oil on canvas, 16"x 20"*

# Victorian Evening

Victorian houses are like old friends; they always seem to welcome your visit! This Victorian house is based on a beautiful structure I observed in rural Connecticut. It had been snowing off and on all morning and my cartoonist friend, Paul Chadwick, and I had been touring small New England villages with our wives in search of vintage architecture. We had stopped at a small cafe renowned for its generous portions (and abundant use of grease!) and were feeling well warmed. Clearly it was time to step outside into the frosty winter air to gather inspiration while loosing body heat! When we came upon this charming two story house, I decided to replace the snow and ice with flowers and foliage, and the result is "Victorian Evening."

Incidentally, while working on this painting, the patriotic fervor surrounding the war with Iraq was at its height. Having already hung an American flag on my porch in support and recognition of the courage of our soldiers, I decided to go a step further and hang a flag on the porch in "Victorian Evening" as well!

*Oil on canvas, 16"x 20"*

# HOMESTEAD HOUSE
## Great American Mansions I

The quiet beauty of things humble. That's been the focus of much of my art. And yet, though I love the tumbledown charm of cottages and country places, I'm also drawn to the more formal beauty of the truly grand estates whose substantial houses are triumphs of world architecture.

I've long wanted to balance my artistic account by celebrating some of these great palatial estates, starting with those located in our own country. Hence "Homestead House", first in my new Great American Mansions series. Nanette and I recently toured the deep South seeking examples of the grand plantation style.

"Homestead House" with its stately Doric columns and imposing facade, framed by lavish magnolias and live oaks hung heavy with Spanish moss, is the very essence of what we found. Here is an estate that would have delighted Scarlett O'Hara and Rhett Butler; indeed, if you look closely, you'll find some familiar initials carved into a tree.

America's great mansions. Very few of us will ever be privileged to live in them. But I invite you to enjoy their sublime beauty in my new series.

*Oil on canvas, 16"x 20"*

# COUNTRY MEMORIES
## The Old Covered Bridge at Thomaston Brook

While visiting New England recently, my wife and I decided to search for some of the old haunts of our mutual hero, Norman Rockwell. While touring Arlington, Vermont, we came upon the house where Rockwell lived during the 40's and 50's. This beautiful old colonial house is located near a tiny covered bridge and is situated on a village green. Behind the house sits the barn-like building Rockwell used as his studio. I was speechless with excitement. Here was the very location where many of Rockwell's best known paintings were created! What's more, upon snooping around, we discovered that the current owners of Rockwell's studio had converted the ample buildings into a charming country inn! We managed with a bit of haggling to reserve Rockwell's studio for the night. That evening, while warming ourselves in front of the fireplace, we could almost imagine Norman Rockwell sitting beside us reminiscing about his painting career.

"Country Memories" is a loving tribute to the charming country area Rockwell called home for so many years. It is also a tribute to the simpler, wholesome era he captured in many of his paintings, when a night out meant a ride in a horse-drawn carriage and a day off meant a trip to the village fishing hole. Incidentally, the village in the background is a compilation of many of the villages we visited on our trip. So, don't be disappointed when you don't see this exact view if you ever visit Norman Rockwell's home territory!

*Oil on canvas, 16"x 20"*

# The Autumn Gate

A gate is an invitation to explore! I spotted this gate while driving through a tiny Cotswold village having just painted the cottage featured in my painting, "McKenna's Cottage." I knew at once I must record the gate in paint, yet since daylight was escaping, I quickly snapped a few reference photos and vowed to recreate the gate in my studio once I returned to America.

Six months later, I began work on "The Autumn Gate" and had the most unusual experience. As I worked on the painting I became intrigued not with the gate itself, but the road that lay beyond! I just couldn't stop imagining where the tiny road led.

Was it to a beautiful wooded estate with a lavish manor house just waiting to be painted. Or perhaps a lush cottage waited beyond with a garden of flowers withering in the chill air of autumn. Funny enough, while standing in England taking photographs of the gate, I had become distracted by a man tending a burning pile of leaves and had never even attempted to see what lay up the road. The mystery beyond the gate became almost an obsession. I had to know what it was. On a later trip to England, I actually returned to the spot, went beyond the gate and painted my delightful discovery in " Beyond Autumn Gate."

*Oil on canvas, 24"x 30"*

# Home Is Where The Heart Is

Like many others, I enjoy the look of charming two-story homes such as this, with shutters on the windows, flower lined walkways, and a shade tree towering over the front lawn. As I worked on this painting, I imagined my own family living in this beautiful setting. Of course, my wife, Nanette, would want white wicker furniture on the covered porches to allow us to enjoy the cool air on summer evenings as we watched our children play. For my three year old daughter, Merritt, a swing is in order, hung from one of the branches of the large front yard tree. My toddler daughter, Chandler, would naturally enjoy playing with her toys as she explored the lawns.

In my painting, I left a teddy bear beneath the tree where it would no doubt remain at day's end. As the children head inside to embark on the rituals of bedtime, the evening guardians of the premises, our cats, keep a careful watch on the yard—especially the birdhouse which hangs from the tree! By the way, the title "Home Is Where The Heart Is" has a double significance; three hearts can be found within the painting, including one carved into the large tree bearing the initials of my wife and I. Those same initials were emblazoned on a similar tree when we were first sweethearts almost twenty years ago!

*Oil on canvas, 20" x 24"*

# Winter's End

For poets, the changing seasons aren't just pages on a calendar; they can be symbols of life's passages from childhood to old age. Remember Robert Frost's famous poem—*Stopping By Woods on a Snowy Evening*—with its enchanted winter woods.

Painters sometimes do pretty much the same thing Mr. Frost did. Yes, my "Winter's End" is about that special time when winter warms into spring. But it's also about the tracks we leave in our passage through life. Sometimes, I like to imagine that the sled which left its trail in the melting snow might be the same one that carried Frost's traveller. Certainly, this evergreen wood, its trees crowned with the snows of a departing winter is "lovely, dark and deep."

For me, the woods are a comfortable place—a memory of a simpler time. Maybe grandmother had her cottage nestled among those protective trees. Life progresses, of course; we have to move on. But the tracks a sled leaves in the snow will never completely disappear—not as long as you have "Winter's End" to keep the memory fresh.

*Oil on canvas, 30"x 40"*

# SWEETHEART COTTAGE II
## A Tranquil Dusk at Falbrooke Thatch

I guess I'm a hopeless romantic—but proud to be one! No series of mine makes that more clear than my "Sweetheart Cottages." For the second work in the series, I've conjured a vision of a perfect romantic hideaway. "Falbrooke Thatch" is nestled right next to a charming little waterfall, with an arched footbridge leading from the front door over the falls. Twilight warms the mist; at nightfall, the sound of falling water will sing a gentle lullaby just for lovers.

This is just the kind of quaint cottage with its stone steps, tidy thatched roof, antique lampposts, and bower of bright flowers where Nanette and I love to go for our frequent second honeymoons. I've devoted "Falbrooke Thatch" to Valentine's Day (note the 214 address just below the heart-shaped window) and to romance. In fact, I've hidden hearts throughout the painting as a tribute to my own sweetheart, Nanette.

*Oil on canvas, 16"x 12"*

# THE BLESSINGS OF AUTUMN
## Blessings of the Seasons I

"The Blessings of Autumn" which begins my new Blessings of the Seasons portfolio was inspired by my recent stay in Norman Rockwell's Arlington, Vermont studio. The white frame house with green shutters is pure New England, as are the rich warm colors so typical of autumn in that area. But in the process of painting, I decided to go beyond the particulars of the scene to attempt capturing the very essence of the season.

Here is the fullness of autumn, the ripe orange plumpness of pumpkins, the Indian corn wreath on the front door, the flaming reds and golds of the maples, the soft blanket of fallen leaves, the brisk clarity of air and light. In this season, nature's promise of abundance is fulfilled; the rigors of winter lie ahead, but we've stored away autumn's rich harvest.

As an artist, I've learned that each season has its special pleasures; each speaks in its own way of God's gracious provision in our lives. I hope you'll share it all with me through my Blessings of the Seasons series.

*Oil on canvas, 18" x 27"*

# The End of a Perfect Day

As much as I love lush gardens and quaint cottages, I also love the unspoiled grandeur of woods and wild places. Paintings like "The End of a Perfect Day" express my growing appreciation for the real beauty of nature untamed.

This rustic stone cabin is nestled in a glorious setting— a secluded jewel of a lake framed by distant mountains and warmed by the golden glow of sunset. Here, the night still belongs to the owls and coyotes whose lonesome voices will soon echo through the evening skies. The cabin is a safe haven, graced with human touches that mark it as a comfortable retreat; a rocking chair on the porch, fishing poles neatly stacked where they've been left after doing combat with rainbow trout. A fireplace warms the living room, illuminating the overstuffed chair and mounted animal trophies glimpsed through open windows.

I'll admit it—even my paintings of nature's wild places often include the charming and comfortable signs of man's presence. Retreating to a lakeside hideaway after a day enjoying the tranquility of nature is my ideal way to end a "perfect day."

*Oil on canvas, 16"x 20"*

# THOMAS KINKADE'S
## Christmas — Celebration of Light

No doubt about it, Christmas is my favorite artistic subject. Undoubtedly, that's because it is, quite simply, my favorite holiday. Its spiritual message, its affirmation of faith, its appeal to our best and most generous instincts, all make it a day like no other. But as I review this collection of my Christmas art, it strikes me that there are some other things about the season that touch me deeply. Family, security, celebration, memories of simpler times, these themes recur in painting after painting.

Christmas is the time when I feel closest to my childhood. I recreate those things that were most important to me thirty years ago; the annual gathering of family, the security of a warm house to enter when frost nipped at my nose, the smell of food cooking and the comfortable, satisfied feeling after the holiday feast, the wonderful tree glowing with lights, and the delightful anticipation as cherished gifts are exchanged.

I suppose I express Christmas memories from my own past by turning the clock back in many of these paintings. Somehow my dream "Kinkade Christmas" would feature such things as horse-drawn sleighs, lamplit walkways, and cozy Victorian houses. It's not that I believe the Yuletide Celebration of Light is a thing of the past. Quite the contrary, I fervently hope that, in a small way, my work will help to encourage these traditions far into the future. In the meantime, please accept as a loving gift from me to you: nostalgic visions of Christmas long ago or yet to be, through heartfelt paintings of "The Celebration of Light".

# Home For the Holidays

I don't know if anyone truly experiences Christmas the way we all picture it. Somehow I think Christmas, like childhood, is a magical blend of reality and imagination. Christmas has always supplied me with a wealth of inspiration. I was fortunate enough to grow up in a small town where Christmas still meant carolling and sleigh rides and snowmen. Those childhood Christmas memories seem to blend and intermingle as the years go by, so that when I paint nostalgic recreations of Christmas past, I can never be sure where experience ends and fantasy begins!

"Home For the Holidays" is an example of memory and imagination blending together to create an idyllic vision. Who hasn't daydreamed about taking a frosty sleigh ride to visit friends for a bit of Christmas Eve cheer? Presents will be exchanged, prayers offered, and perhaps a mug of steaming punch will send you on your way.

By the way, my three year old daughter, Merritt, is a wonderful model for paintings like this. In tribute to her efforts, her name adorns the mailbox to the right of the sleigh.

*Oil on canvas, 16"x 20"*

# Christmas Eve

One of the great pleasures of Christmas is that each holiday is new, fresh, joyous. And yet each is also a reminder of Christmases past, a connection to our best memories of home and family. That's just the way the paintings in my "Christmas Cottage" series work. This series, which has become one of my most popular, is planned as an annual event that will extend from 1990 through the turn of the century, Lord willing! Each year's addition stands on its own, and yet each adds to my growing portrayal of the joys of a favorite season. Like its companion pieces,

"ChristmasEve" features a small address placard in the right foreground bearing the release year "1991" as if it were the address of the cottage.

"Christmas Eve" is, plain, simple, and an expression of my ongoing love affair with the Christmas season. This wonderful old stone cottage allows me to express the lights, mood, and magic of the most wonderful season of the year. As is so often true in my paintings, the tiny "N" adorning the sign beside the door is a tribute to Nanette, my wife.

*Oil on canvas, 12"x 16"*

# Evening Carolers

This painting celebrates one of the most universal Christmas traditions: the singing of joyous Christmas carols. There's nothing that lifts the spirit like joining in song with those you love on a crisp December evening.

I painted the house portion of this painting directly from a beautiful house in the Cotswold district of England. I knew that its special dignity and warmth made it the perfect setting for some sort of celebration, but at the time I wasn't sure just what.

When I returned home an inspiration hit me. I decided to introduce a Christmas theme and added the figures of the carolers. The fact that this painting was created in two separate countries is appropriate. After all, Christmas caroling is one tradition that is truly international in scope.

*Oil on canvas, 8"x 10"*

# Home for the Evening

The title of this tiny painting was originally "Cookies Baking." As I worked on the piece, I could almost smell the sweet aroma of homemade cookies coming from inside the snow covered cottage. I finished the painting, put a brass nameplate on the frame that said "Cookies Baking", and sent the piece to an art show in Texas. As the miniature print was being made I had forgotten the sensation of smelling cookies, and had begun to feel something broader from the piece. I eventually isolated that feeling: it was a nostalgic sense of home. To me the painting simply said, "being home." Perhaps it was because about that time my wife and I were expecting Chandler, our second daughter. Or perhaps it was because we were remodeling our home right about then. Whatever the cause, the painting became "Home for the Evening" in my mind, and has stayed so ever since.

By the way, the number "5282" that appears on the mailbox in front of the cottage is a tribute to one of my favorite dates, May 2, 1982—the day my wife, Nanette, and I were married. As an artist, I have an advantage over most husbands; hiding my anniversary date in my paintings helps me to never forget what it is!

*Oil on canvas, 8"x 10"*

# Christmas Cottage

Christmas has always been my favorite holiday. I think that, as an artist, I especially enjoy the visual aspects of Christmas—the crisp, snowy mornings, strands of colored lights adorning trees and buildings, the feeling of hearth and home. My Christmas Cottage series is my way of annually celebrating in paint the season I love most, complete with all the visual aspects I enjoy so much. And as I often find, the things that I enjoy painting are often the things that many others enjoy viewing! This is especially true of my Christmas paintings. It's as though each of us share the same inner daydream of our ideal Christmas. In fact, the best compliment I could receive is for collectors of the series to tell me, "I wish I could be there this Christmas!" I hope everyone who sees the Christmas Cottage series will consider these paintings as a heartfelt Christmas gift from one romantic to another!

*Oil on canvas, 12"x 16"*

# Silent Night

In this, the third of my annual Christmas releases, I painted a theme I find particularly satisfying:  The peaceful reverence of a moonlit Christmas Eve. In fact, this is the first moonlit cottage I've ever put into print. I was so taken with the simple message of the classic Christmas carol "Silent Night", with its beautiful images of sleeping villages and the coming of the Christ child, that I decided to give this annual Christmas release the same title and to evoke a bit of the song's mood. What could be more enchanting than a full moon on Christmas Eve with the stars beside the moon shining down on a sleeping, snow-covered village?

I hope this painting will remind each of us of the message of hope and peace that is the *true* meaning of Christmas as illustrated in the Savior's birth.

*Oil on canvas, 12"x 16"*

# St. Nicholas Circle

I began to work on this painting in Norman Rockwell's great studio near Arlington, Vermont. I was captivated by the charming New England architecture; many of the little gems in surrounding towns made their way into "St. Nicholas Circle."

This is nothing less than my dream Christmas village—in this one idyllic spot time stands still, and it's Christmas all year 'round. The heart of town is the skating pond and Christmas tree; the church and town hall, the shops and homes circle the pond like wreathes. Horse-drawn sleighs are the only transport, the little lanes have fanciful holiday names, lights and bows deck the trees, and snowmen stand vigil on the hillside. Is there anything more enchanting than the thought of Christmas all year 'round?

*Oil on canvas, 16"x 20"*

# STONEHEARTH HUTCH
## Christmas Cottage IV

One of the things I enjoy about the great Renaissance Painters is the fact that they had a language of symbols to work with—a broad vocabulary of visual cues their audience was sure to understand.

That's one reason I'm drawn to Christmas as a subject for my art — the symbols of the season speak very clearly to us all. I've incorporated some of them — wreath and tree — in "Stonehearth Hutch", fourth in my Christmas Cottage series, to signal that the warm glow of this sunset heralds Christmas Eve.

I've also used more personal symbols to express the spirit of the season. The lone, rough-hewn stone cottage represents the rock of faith. Outside is only the solitude of the woods —with no carriage track or footprint to hint at human comfort. But inside is a golden light, suggesting the hope of Christmas. Fires burn in each hearth, promising abundant food; their smoke rises heavenward. The odd little path, winding and slippery, leads to the cottage door.

My prayer is that "Stonehearth Hutch" will communicate to many, in a language as universal as Christmas wreaths, yet as deeply as faith.

*Oil on canvas, 12"x 16"*

# Victorian Christmas

Some homes just beg to be painted! This stately old Victorian stands on a prominent street corner in my home town. Since I was a young boy, I've been fascinated with the unusual asymmetrical design and carpenter's gothic touches, or "gingerbread" of the home.

I decided to turn back the clock to Christmas Eve around the turn of the century. I imagined the festivities surrounding a Christmas Eve open house, with guests coming and going and mischievous children frolicking in the snow. I pictured the beautiful old house all lit up for the occasion, with the glow from the windows cascading down the snowy hill.

Just for fun, I included some whimsical touches. For instance, the man smoking a pipe in the lower left hand corner is none other than Norman Rockwell. The nostalgic activities of the scene seemed something Rockwell would have enjoyed, so I couldn't resist including him!

*Oil on canvas, 20"x 24"*

# Victorian Christmas II

Christmas parties. I've been to some wonderfully festive affairs and I imagine you have, too. But today, I'm inviting you to a Christmas party unlike any you have ever attended, because it takes place a hundred years ago!

The "party" is being held at a very stately Victorian mansion, which you might be able to locate in Placerville, the northern California town where I grew up. But I welcome you to look for that grand historical house instead in my new painting "Victorian Christmas II." The festivities are in full swing as you arrive. Guests have tethered their horses or handed them over to the carriage house attendant. At the top of the stone walkway, your hosts await to greet you while boisterous children slide gleefully on their sleds. Above it all, the grand house is ablaze with holiday lights.

In my paintings, I love turning back the clock to a simpler era. That's what my Victorian Christmas series is all about; it brings my favorite holiday and a glorious historical period alive on canvas.

*Oil on canvas, 20" x 24"*

# Catalog Raisonné of Published Works, 1983—1993

Afternoon Light, Dogwood
Amber Afternoon
Artist's Point, Yosemite
Auburn
The Autumn Gate
Beside Still Waters
Beyond Autumn Gate
Birth Of A City
The Blessings of Autumn
Blossom Hill Church
Blue Cottage
Boston
The Broadwater Bridge, Thomashire
Carmel, Dolores Street
Carmel, Ocean Avenue
Cedar Nook Cottage

Chandler's Cottage
Christmas at the Ahwahnee
Christmas at the Courthouse
Christmas Cottage
Christmas Eve
Christmas On Main Street
Cottage By The Sea
Country Memories
Dawson
The End of A Perfect Day
Entrance to the Manor House
Evening at Merritt's Cottage
Evening at Swanbrooke Cottage
Evening Carolers
Evening Service
Flags Over The Capitol

The Garden of Promise
The Garden Party
Glory of Evening
Glory of Morning
Heather's Hutch
Hemet
The Hidden Cottage
The Hidden Cottage II
Home for the Evening
Home For the Holidays
Home Is Where The Heart Is
Homestead House
The Ice Harvest
Julianne's Cottage
Lamplight Lane
Light Unto My Path